Evans Modern T

Reading and Reading Failures

Evans Modern Teaching

Reading and Reading Failures

John M. Hughes

Evans Brothers Limited London

Published by Evans Brothers Limited
Montague House,
Russell Square, London WC1

By the same author:
Aids to Reading
Beginning Reading
Phonics and the Teaching of Reading
Reading with Phonics

Artwork by Vanda Morton

Filmset in 11 on 12 Imprint by
Photoprint Plates Limited, Rayleigh, Essex
and printed in Great Britain by
T. & A. Constable Ltd., Edinburgh
ISBN 0 237 28194 5   PRA 4233

Contents

List of Tables

Introduction

Is there any justification for the amount of effort and time that we devote to the teaching of reading when there has been this tremendous swing towards the visual and oral communication of television, radio, the telephone, the tape recorder, the public address system and even notices on which images are now becoming more important than words? Are we really wasting our time by teaching to some children what *some* people regard as an outmoded communication medium? After all, there are many people who hardly ever read, except to find the minimum of information—the names of the runners in the three o'clock at Epsom or the times of TV programmes. It is believed that, nationally, about 5 per cent of children are unable to read or write a letter at eleven-plus. Probably the figure may be as high as 35 per cent in certain inner urban areas. On the other hand, however, we have the person who relies on his ability to read as a form of relaxation and to read for information and so provide his daily bread.

Surely reading can provide something unique, if only an opportunity to have another opinion, additional information or pleasure. Enjoyment and pleasure must surely be placed high on the list. We cannot all have similar tastes, behaviour, attitudes and occupations, but we cannot assume that a child will not require the ability to read, no matter what difficulty he finds in attaining this skill. Are we to decide which children, aged between five and eight years, will require reading in later life and which will not? We must ensure that all children are given the opportunity to learn to read, regardless of the possibility that many will turn away from reading and rely more or less exclusively on the visual and oral mass media rather than on the printed word.

Reading is a 'tool' subject in that, if a child is unable to read, he suffers from serious handicaps not only in school but in later life. Here we are living in an age of 'child-centred' education, so called 'progressive approaches' and 'discovery methods', all placing a far greater emphasis on a child's ability to read. Reading ability is essential if a child is to complete his 'assignment cards'; if he is to carry out his 'recordings' correctly, and if he is to 'discover' for himself from glossy and expensive reference books as well as from the 'Ladybird-type' books. If we believe in this 'modern approach' for our children then *we must not neglect the acquisition of reading skills* in order that our children benefit fully from this approach. Too many 'educationists' believe (and even advise) that reading is something that can be acquired incidentally. They advise teachers to allow their children to discover reading and not to force them along too quickly—'they will read when they are ready'. Yes, some children do appear to learn to read quite incidentally. Yes, some children do appear to discover reading for themselves. *But* many of these are children who will read *in spite of the teacher*. Many of these children were reading before they entered school. We are all aware of the effect of a 'good home background', *but* are we also aware of the effects of a culturally deprived home background?

Children, generally, require systematic teaching which should be based on the diagnosis of their individual needs. Many children will not acquire the necessary reading skills if left to their own devices. In this era of 'non-streaming', it is almost a certainty that a teacher will have a number of children in her class experiencing reading difficulties. Are teachers prepared to provide effective learning situations that cater for a wide range of ability? For example, are they prepared to cater for the needs of a class of top juniors with reading ages ranging from six to fourteen plus years?

There is official literature available which suggests that reading attainments have improved since the early Fifties (*Progress in Reading*, 1966 and *The Plowden Report*, 1967), but there are still too many children with inadequate reading attainments. A considerable number of children are either failing to learn to read, or are mastering only the bare mechanics. The results of thirteen years' research into reading standards by Dr Morris (1966) showed that in Kent one out of eight children is unable to read by the age of eight. She found that half of these were only semi-literate by the end of their school days. Her survey showed that about 45 per cent of seven thousand children still needed teaching methods related to those of the infant school when they transferred to junior school, although 75 per cent of the teachers who received them had had no infant school experience, and 18 per cent had no knowledge of how to begin to teach children to read. Many children who cannot read when they reach junior school are severely prejudiced in their chances of making a success of their future school careers. Unfortunately, there are too many children who fall into this category. /

Recent surveys provide some insight into the amount of importance attached to the training of students, in Colleges of Education, for the teaching of reading. During her Kent survey, Dr Morris found that interviews with junior school teachers suggested that the discrepancy between the demands of their task and their equipment for it lay partly in the fact that, in college, they had not usually been made sufficiently aware of their role as potential teachers of reading and given the appropriate instruction and practice in teaching juniors to read. Many of these teachers started their careers thinking that they would rarely have to cope with pupils who could not read.

In 1968 Cortis and Dean carried out a survey amongst probationary teachers in Berkshire. 35 per cent claimed that they had no methodical training and encouragement in regard to the techniques of teaching reading. In the same year, Dr Elizabeth Goodacre (*Times Educational Supplement*, 27 February 1970) carried out a survey involving 350 teachers in one of the home counties and a Midland city. 24 per cent of the group of probationary teachers and infant teachers were dissatisfied about the instruction they had received on the teaching of reading and 11 per cent were satisfied. But 20 per cent of those who had qualified in the last five years (1963–68) claimed that they had received no training in preparation for the teaching of reading. 40 per cent of these teachers claimed that the training was very limited indeed, frequently consisting of a lecture or two, an essay and a reading list. When these teachers were asked to give more information about their courses, the majority claimed that they had covered general psychological principles of learning in relation to reading and about three-quarters claimed that their courses had dealt with reading methods, but only half had covered remedial work.

A survey carried out by the National Union of Teachers (National Young Teachers Advisory Committee) in 1969 asked 560 newly qualified infant and junior teachers whether their college training had included the teaching of reading. 17 per cent claimed that the teaching of reading had not been included *at all* and 29 per cent stated that where it was included it was covered inadequately. About 25 per cent were satisfied with their course. In the same year, a survey was carried out in London (the London literacy survey), and this generally confirmed the findings of the other surveys. Very few teachers in London had received specific or detailed training in the teaching of reading.

Schools and teachers must take some responsibility for the poor reading ability of quite a proportion of their pupils. It is the teacher who needs, and often asks for, advice on the teaching of reading, and it is essential that the necessary requirements are met. Unfortunately, there are some teachers who do not take advantage of the facilities and courses offered to them. Frequently these are teachers who have never taken an interest in the *actual* teaching of reading and do not wish to because the majority of their children are reading and the others 'are too dull to read'.

Fault must surely be placed on the training that college of education students receive. It appears obvious that an essential part of a primary school course (and I am not forgetting the secondary school course) should be the teaching of reading, and students should have the opportunity of acquiring the necessary knowledge to diagnose and treat reading disability. I fully appreciate that much has been achieved over recent years and that there has been significant expansion of reading courses at Colleges of Education, Departments of Education and In-service courses. Many local education authorities, organisers, advisers and teachers have made tremendous efforts to tackle the problem and 'plug the gap'. Much has been done—*but there is much more to do.*

It is hoped that this book, in some small way, will further help to 'plug the gap'. It does not purport to present in detail all that a student or teacher should know about the teaching of reading and the many problems associated with the topic. It is, however, a comprehensive guide or handbook that may serve to encourage all those concerned with the teaching of reading to study aspects of the problem in more depth, and to give more thought to the responsibility which rests in their hands. It is hoped that a study of the various suggestions and guides, and of the advice given, will lead the reader on to the provision of further approaches and innovations. The book does, however, make a plea for a more systematic and direct approach to the teaching of reading and places particular emphasis on the teaching of phonics which, in the opinion of the author, has been sadly neglected in the past. If this book leads to a fuller appreciation of the problem and a re-evaluation of existing practices in many classrooms throughout the land, then its aim will have been achieved.

Chapter 1

Teaching reading:
a short historical background

Of all the skills taught at school, reading can be regarded as a 'tool' skill, in the sense that a child's progress in other subjects will depend considerably on his reading ability. It cannot be over-emphasised, therefore, that reading failure is a major factor in educational failure. Reading has come to hold *the* most significant place in education as a means of communication in a highly literate society. Thus the teaching of reading is of the utmost importance to parents and teachers. Reading requires a stimulating environment to arouse and maintain motivation. Those concerned with helping the child to read must have the necessary knowledge of the methods of teaching reading so that the ultimate goal—to help the child to help himself—is achieved.

It is a sad fact that, one hundred years after the first Education Act of 1870 which introduced compulsory education with government aid in England and Wales, one can still find the illiterate, the semi-literate and the functionally illiterate in this country, and these are not only the mentally handicapped.

From the days of the Ancient Greeks until well into the nineteenth century, the alphabet dominated the early teaching of reading. It appears that the first main objective of the teacher was to teach the child to recognise and name the letters of the alphabet, both capital and small, in alphabetical order. There is evidence to suggest that from about the ninth century onwards there was an emphasis on the spelling out of pronounceable combinations of letters. In many cases, these combinations were based on the use of the Bible.

The first hornbooks appeared in 1415. The hornbook consisted of one sheet in a wooden frame covered with transparent horn. Up to about 1800, hornbooks were commonly used, and for some considerable time printed primers followed the pattern that was set by these hornbooks. The common hornbook in

England had the cross of Christ in the top left-hand corner, the alphabet in both small and capital letters, columns of ab, eb, ob syllables and the Lord's Prayer. When the child could recognise the single letters, he then moved on to the learning of two-letter combinations, and some of these would be incorporated in short sentences. He then progressed to three-letter combinations and so on. The fact that the syllables were in the hornbook is of considerable significance in appreciating the process by which the child learned to read. Words were spelled out and memorised. The fact that the printed letters sounded within a word had different sounds when spelled out was criticised by many teachers, but this method must have been quite successful, since it was in use for some considerable time.

A very dull situation must have prevailed during the first four decades of the nineteenth century when monitors instructed regimented pupils in the spelling out of syllables and words. But although children learned to read by spelling out the letters within words, there is no doubt that children became aware of the configuration of words, and the basis of both 'whole word' and 'phonic' methods must surely have been present.

There were several attempts to ease the process of alphabetic learning. During the eighteenth century the 'gingerbread' method became fashionable. Hornbooks made of gingerbread were given to children to encourage them to learn their letters. It was suggested at this time that learning is best enjoyed once the child had learned his letters and he had the pleasure of eating them. But until well into the nineteenth century, in both England and America, the teaching of reading was associated with the alphabet and spelling, using the Bible as the text.

Manuscripts of over four hundred years ago contained many variations in spelling. These different spellings were generally accepted. Standard spelling was gradually established with the compilation of dictionaries. In 1783 Noah Webster, an American, published the *Blue-Backed Speller* in the United States. This was the most popular reading primer in the United States for over a hundred years. It gradually replaced the *New England Primer* which had been based on the alphabetic method. Webster's primer offered a phonic method.

Phonic methods began to make an impact in England in the middle of the nineteenth century but they did not displace the alphabetic method until some time after the change-over was accomplished in the United States. However, substantial progress

8

was made following the establishment of Kay-Shuttleworth's training college for teachers at Battersea.

The mid-nineteenth century saw an emergence of 'sounding out' books. Most of the original phonic methods taught the sounds of letters first, beginning with the more usual ones such as the short vowels and some of the consonants. Early reading material consisted of short words with regular pronunciations. The words used could be analysed into constituent sounds and then resynthesised to form the word in a regular way. Attempts to produce simpler spelling in order to make the learning of reading easier were tried out. (Isaac Pitman's alphabet was tried out in the United States.) The 'payment by results' system in the latter part of the nineteenth century resulted in teachers concentrating on getting their pupils through examinations. So this became a period of sheer rote learning and drill.

But there were many critics of the phonic method in the nineteenth century and these advocated a different approach— the 'look and say' approach. Critics of the phonic method argued that children do not tackle words or sentences in an analytic manner. They suggested that to start with individual sounds was an unnatural way of relating the spoken language, with which the child was already familiar, to the written form which he had to learn to read and write. It was, therefore, suggested that whole words should be used linked with objects and pictures which the child would learn to recognise because they were relevant to his experiences. At this time the 'whole word' approach was regarded as synonymous with the 'look and say' approach.

But it was not until well into the twentieth century that the phonic method was seriously threatened by the 'whole word' method. Many educationists began to suggest that if children do not normally read by spelling out the word, very little is gained by teaching them sounds and letters as the first steps of reading. It was suggested that it was probably more beneficial to show the word and tell the child what it is. This is particularly appropriate when the sound of the word is already familiar. It was postulated, therefore, that a child would attend to words or groups of words that were meaningful to him—and because some of these words might be long or phonically irregular, it was not possible in any case to teach them using a phonic method.

Towards the end of the nineteenth century, the 'sentence' method began to be considered in the British Isles. The main influence towards sentence methods came from Belgium as a result of the work of Decroly. From 1912 onwards, Gestaltan psychology appeared to add justification to the method of presenting whole words or sentences. The Gestalt theory lent its authority to the practice of teaching an alphabetically printed language by encouraging word recognition before attempting to break down words into their individual sounds and before acquiring the main rules for English spelling and pronunciation. It was suggested that only when children could identify many different words, either contained in their own vocabularies and written for them by the teacher, or from various series of reading primers, did it become necessary to teach phonic analysis. The writers of reading books concentrated on producing books with as small a vocabulary as possible. The words were repeated as often as possible without ruining the story. Vocabulary control was used. The proponents of 'look and say' stated that phonic methods produced readers who 'barked at print' and comprehension was adversely affected, whereas 'look and say' encouraged fluency and understanding.

Many teachers compromised by using an approach called 'mixed methods'. Here whole words or sentences were used but the children's attention was drawn to individual letter sounds within the words.

During the ten years following the Second World War, the teaching of reading came very much to the foreground. The selection procedures of the British Forces discovered a large number of people who either could not read at all, or who were categorised as 'functionally illiterate'. The functionally illiterate did not have the necessary skill in reading and writing to read and fill in 'everyday' forms.

In 1947 the Government set up a committee 'to consider the nature and extent of the illiteracy alleged to exist among school leavers and young people and, if necessary, to make recommendations'. The committee suggested that reading material should be 'word' and not 'letter' based.

During recent years there appears to have been a swing of the pendulum. Certain educationists have suggested that children taught through the phonic method learn to read more effectively and tackle new material with more confidence. So a 'phonic revolt' has taken place. In 1958 Terman and Walcutt in America stated that teaching words as meaningful wholes ignores the basic fact that 'printed words are symbols of sounds and are made up of letters which are symbols of sounds'. Flesch's book

10

Why Johnny Can't Read created a great amount of concern in the United States because it was extremely critical of the 'look and say' method. But this book also received criticism because it appeared to advocate a return to the old-fashioned phonic method. After all, it appears that the earlier rejection of the alphabetic and phonic methods was because of the monotonous drill involved. But probably children themselves had the most substantial reason for the rejection of these methods because while they are being shown why the word 'dog' is printed as it is, they are learning and reading with no apparent difficulty such words as 'aeroplane', 'space-ship' and 'elephant'.

During the last thirty years, a growing body of opinion has suggested that the differentiation and identification of letter shapes and words should not be taught in isolation. For example, in Daniels and Diack's *Royal Road Readers* the approach involves a phonic word method.

The phonic method of teaching reading has been criticised because the English language contains so many inconsistencies and many attempts have been made to overcome the fact that sounds and symbols do not have a consistent one-to-one correlation. There have been many attempts to overcome the problem of presenting children with predictably regular ways of decoding words. One way is to mark letters in words in such a way that children can easily discover how certain letters are pronounced in a particular context. Systems are used that do not attempt to change the actual letters or ordering of letters in words. They are merely props used as aids in the deciphering of a code. These props are gradually dropped as the child learns to read without difficulty. One system uses diacritical marks, another uses colour cues, and the initial teaching alphabet is an approach which involves the changing or adding of letters to represent certain sounds.

When certain children experience difficulty in learning to read there may be a variety of reasons, but it is possible that the method used is simply unsuitable for these particular children. Some children have poor visual memories and are unable to remember words as wholes. Other children have poor auditory discrimination and experience difficulty with phonic analysis.

Flexibility, versatility and ingenuity are essential to the successful teaching of reading because of the individual differences in the way children learn to read. I would not suggest that one method is absolutely superior to another because I have found that any method, practice or approach is likely to work better with some children than with others. It is the teacher who has the greatest influence on a child's progress in reading and the most important criterion involved in the teaching of reading is not so much the method being adopted but the individual teacher's faith and enthusiasm in the method she is using.

Chapter 2

Methods of teaching reading

There is much controversy over the best method of teaching reading because the method or methods used successfully with some children are found to be inadequate with others. It is the teacher's responsibility to discover where each child's weaknesses lie and to be sufficiently acquainted with the various methods in order to choose and use the most appropriate. A brief discussion of the various methods of teaching reading is of the utmost importance in order that we, as teachers or parents, have a better understanding of the problems involved. (An extremely useful book is *Reading—Which approach?* ULP.)

'Whole word' or 'look and say' method

It has been suggested that the 'whole word' method should be separated from the 'look and say' method, but there is so much overlapping of these two that it is more advantageous to discuss them under one heading.

These methods are based on an approach which emphasises that children should learn a number of words as 'sight words' before attempting any form of word analysis. This method also ensures that the introduction of sight words is controlled. Often children learn these words as visual patterns before they are taught the names and sounds of the letters making up the words.

The arguments put forward for the use of this method include the following:

    a In the initial stages of learning to read it is easier for a child to learn sight words than it is to learn the rules of phonic analysis and synthesis, considering the many exceptions to the rules. Many of the exceptions are 'service words', e.g. are, the, you, here and what, and they are found in all reading material.

b Learning words as 'wholes' leads to whole word perception, which is regarded as more beneficial than seeing the word as a pattern made up of a number of parts.

c A child can be helped to see and hear similarities between the known sight words and new words. A sight vocabulary, therefore, helps him to unlock new words.

d If a child learns words as 'wholes' then he should be conditioned to look at all of the word. This should help the child in reading phrases and sentences because he looks at the first word and moves through the others from left to right.

e Reading is more meaningful when words are learned and read in logical sequence. Often pictorial representation can be an additional clue.

In the early stages of reading, many children find it easier to recognise words by sight rather than by building them up from letter sounds. Many words are learned by sight through the use of flash cards. The teacher has a set of standard-sized cards with single words printed on them. She may help the child learn the word by showing it to him and telling him what it says. She then asks the child to say it. She then tells the child to have a good look at the word and try to remember it. After a period of time, the teacher shows the card again and asks the child what it says. This is done with several cards but the teacher ensures that the child is continually revising the previous ones. The cards are shown systematically but when a child appears to have learned the words in this particular order, the teacher shuffles the cards and shows them to the child in a random order. If a child does not remember a word, the teacher repeats the learning procedure for that one card. More cards are gradually introduced but the 'known' words are still included. Many games may be devised to help the child learn these words (see *Aids to Reading* by J. M. Hughes, Evans Brothers, 1970). If the teacher finds that a child has difficulty in learning certain words, then she may emphasise certain characteristics of the words.

The teacher may also use cards showing pictures with the appropriate words printed underneath. The same words are printed on cards without the illustrations and these are matched with the picture/word cards. The teacher may use cards with pictures on one side and the word on the reverse side. She encourages the child eventually to read the word without having to turn over and look at the picture. It is important that the teacher ensures that the words being learned are meaningful to the child and are within his everyday conversation. The significance of learning the words becomes apparent when the child encounters these words in his reading book. Many teachers ensure that all the words in each reading book are learned before the child is given the book. Thus the child should be able to read the book without much difficulty. This initial success engenders further success.

This method is based on the conception that children see words as whole patterns. They learn to associate the printed word with meaning. Children, therefore, memorise the look of words. This may be achieved because of the word's overall pattern but more frequently it is because of certain details contained in the printed word. Diack (1960) suggests that if a child has no previous information as to which word to expect, he will see particular details before he sees the whole word. Schonell suggested that the 'total pattern' of a word is the most critical factor in identifying words. But when the eye passes over a line of print there is a succession of movements and pauses. Therefore it is likely that some significant small part of the word triggers off a response for the child.

Reading is based on the recognition of symbols. In order to read with fluency and comprehension, a child must increase his level of ability in word recognition. A level should be reached with certain words so that his response becomes almost automatic. At the beginning stage of reading, a child should build up a sight vocabulary of words in common usage in everyday speech. He may use any one of the following means of recognising words and frequently will adopt a combination of two or more:

a   The pattern of the word
b   The length of the word
c   The initial letter of the word
d   The final letter of the word
e   Letter groupings, e.g. 'oo' as in 'look'
f   Contextual clues.

There is no doubt that word pattern is a very important factor in distinguishing between words. The ability to see characteristics in words is an important step in visual discrimination.

This method, therefore, emphasises the shapes of words and it is suggested that, at first, children are not concerned with letters as such. The method involves as many meaningful words as possible, often with pictorial representation as additional aids.

15

It is used to teach many phonically irregular words such as are, the, you, etc.

There is a danger, however, that individual letters may be overlooked and indiscriminate guessing may result. The main disadvantage of using 'look and say' as the *sole* method of teaching reading is that it does not contain a technique for attempting unfamiliar words, so children are unable to work as independently as they should. Many children are unable to learn many whole words at a time and, as a result, much reading material has been produced with strictly limited vocabularies. A great amount of repetition is necessary and there is a danger that certain materials may involve much mechanical drill and become as boring as the alphabetic and phonic methods of the past.

The sentence method

Here the emphasis is on whole sentences and phrases. This method may be regarded as a logical evolution from the 'look and say'/'whole word' method. The proponents of the method suggest that even words cannot give much information in themselves, but a short sentence is more meaningful. The theory is that children should learn words in sentences because sentences are the units of thought. Thus children's interests can be utilised and more attractive reading materials can be provided resulting in rapid and fluent reading. But surely it is not true that meaning is to be found only in sentences. Children see many isolated words which *do* have meaning because they imply sentences, e.g. school (Here is the school), door (This is a door).

There is a danger that if this method is adopted to the exclusion of others or a 'mixed approach', individual letters and words may be excluded or ignored and this may lead to indiscriminate guessing. Also, the method requires frequent repetition of words and the vocabulary of reading materials may be restricted.

The kinaesthetic method

This is a method described by Grace Fernald (1943) and used by teachers for over forty years. It is frequently used with retarded readers, but there is no reason why it should not be incorporated into a 'mixed approach'.

The method employs an 'experience' or 'interest' approach. The child is asked to choose a word which he thinks is difficult. The teacher writes the word in large writing on a piece of paper, saying each syllable as she writes. The child traces over the word with his forefinger and, at the same time, pronounces the syllables of the word. The tracing and vocalisation of the word are repeated until the child feels that he can reproduce it without looking at it. When he has written the word on another piece of paper, and is satisfied that he knows its details, he may be asked to show his ability to the class by writing the word on the blackboard. This method of learning new words involves the visual—auditory—tactile—kinaesthetic modes of learning. It must be remembered, however, that the tracing should be with the forefinger. A pencil should not be used because this impedes the child's 'feel' of the word using the tactile and kinaesthetic senses.

Eventually, the child produces his own reading material and he writes stories about his interests. These will vary in length, and any words he does not know are written by the teacher and are learned by tracing and vocalisation. The finished stories are reprinted by the teacher who makes the occasional correction to grammar and spelling mistakes. The teacher's printed version of the child's story is pasted into the child's 'reading book'. He is asked to read the story aloud to the teacher and then, to the class. Eventually, the need for tracing and vocalisation gradually disappears. The child's confidence is reinforced as his 'reading book' grows in story content. There are always 'normal' reading books available for the child if he wishes to use them. When he moves on to reading printed books, he is encouraged to underline lightly those words which he cannot read. The teacher reads the word and the child learns the word by tracing and vocalisation, then he writes it down without copying from the book. Finally, he reads the text.

One of the most important factors involved in the Kinaesthetic method is the motivational factor. The child reads words based on his own interests and/or experiences and these words come directly from the child. This method combines reading, writing and spelling, and it can be used by the teacher in a most flexible way for many children. The constant tracing and saying of parts of words help the child to understand word construction. The method is based upon the child's creation of his own reading material and there is no dependence upon reading books.

The linguistic approach

The linguistic approach stresses the undesirability of teaching children to isolate the separate sounds of words and then trying to blend these sounds into words. Bloomfield and Barnhart (1961) and Fries (1962) have suggested that the introduction of words can be so arranged that only the entirely regular spellings of sounds are introduced to children in the early stages. Fries states that single-letter-to-sound correspondence just does not work for most words in the English language. However, when he discusses a progression for developing recognition of spelling patterns—simple letter-to-sound correspondences are used.

Fries suggests that the initial stage of the linguistic approach should involve the learning of the visual presentation of letters. He stresses that this should *not* involve the names of letters or sounds and there should be no written work. Many recognition exercises are given to the child using capital letters and they are introduced according to the way in which they are made. He states that the letters should be learned in three separate groups. The grouping depending on the basis of similarity of construction such as:

a letters with straight strokes, e.g. I, T, L, F, E, etc.
b letters with strokes and parts of circles, e.g. D, B, J, U, etc.
c circle letters, e.g. O, Q, S, etc.

The children are taught left/right orientation by giving them exercises to distinguish between I T and T I, E F and F E, etc., and then F I T and T I F, etc.

At the first stage of reading, children are encouraged to respond in a speedy and automatic way to the spelling patterns of English. The whole word is spoken but the individual letters are not sounded, e.g. A T—C A T, C A T—R A T, F A T—H A T, etc. These words should be meaningful ones and should be within the child's language experience.

The second stage is regarded as the productive reading stage. Here stress is placed on reading with understanding; this being brought about by intonation and expression in the actual reading.

The third stage—vivid imaginative realisation—is reached when reading becomes automatic and stimulates creative as well as critical evaluation. At this stage, the child can assimilate and appreciate new experiences. A tremendous amount of time has to be spent on drill and one wonders whether this is not just a

18

return to an approach similar to the old phonic method of years ago. (A critical evaluation of the linguistic approach can be found in 'The Linguistic Approach to Reading' by J. E. Merritt [1964], in *The Third International Reading Symposium*, Cassell.)

The alphabetic method

Children learned the names of letters, AY, BEE, CEE and spelled the names into words, BEE AY TEE says BAT. We are inclined to be very cynical about this method, but many children learned to read, and to read with reasonable efficiency by using it. This method, therefore, emphasised the names and shapes of letters and no doubt helped the learning of letter sequences, left to right word attack and spelling. It was thought that if children saw letters in their normal order in words, and if they were called out often enough, they would learn to read because the names of many consonants suggest their sounds.

This method must surely be difficult and very uninteresting since it consists of drill rather than meaningful reading. Because the names of many letters are often different from the sounds they represent in words, it must have been difficult for children to appreciate that letters are symbols of certain sounds. The fact that one letter may stand for several sounds makes it even more difficult.

The phonic method

This approach to the teaching of reading is based on the relationship of sound and letter. During the nineteenth century the approach to the phonic method began by teaching the child the alphabet. The usual procedure was to draw the child's attention to the form of the printed letter and then tell him the sound that it made. Unfortunately, the approach was to associate a strange letter with a meaningless sound. Consonant sounds rarely occur in language without having a vowel sound appended.

The sound 'ber' which is the usual way of describing the sound for 'b' (in 'bat') does not truly illustrate the sound for 'b'. Many consonants are very difficult to pronounce unless a vowel is involved with them. There is a danger that the phonic method may involve meaningless drill and children may concentrate so much on sound that comprehension may be ignored. But

19

there is no reason why a phonic method should involve such an approach. In the past, writers of beginning reading books produced much artificial reading material and the vocabulary was limited in both <u>words and meaning</u>.

The use of phonics for teaching elementary reading has been criticised by many educationists, when used during this stage of reading, for developing wrong eye movements; it has no meaning for young children; it is psychologically unsound because we see 'wholes' before we are aware of parts; it affects the process of silent reading; it is limited because of the inconsistencies of English spelling and, if phonics are used too soon, children are easily discouraged and lose confidence. It has even been suggested that phonics should be regarded as a technique of word analysis and synthesis and not as a method of teaching reading and that phonic skills develop gradually as children reach a certain level of mental maturity.

People have realised over the last twenty-five years that the differentiation and identification of letter shapes and sounds should not be taught in isolation. For example, in Daniels and Diack's *Royal Road Readers,* the approach involves a phonic word method. The method is based on the idea that material for teaching reading ought to be designed so as to give the child, in as easy a manner as possible, insight into the nature of letters. In the *Royal Road Reading Scheme,* the child does not learn the letters in isolation but functioning in words.

Montessori's approach to the teaching of reading

The teacher sits beside the child and places a pair of sandpaper letters on the desk or table. The first pair of letters are vowels (e.g. a and e). She clearly makes the sound represented by each letter in turn as she traces it by running her finger over the letter. The child learns the correct way to trace the letter by imitation and hears the sound clearly. As a result of this lesson the child is able to select the right letter when the sounds are made and is able to reproduce the sound required when either of the letters is represented. The child carries out further practice alone and fixes the correct movement for tracing and the association of sound with movement and visual impression. The tracing is continued even after the child has begun to write on the blackboard or on paper because of the help that this gives in perfecting the writing.

Individual lessons reveal the abilities of each child. If the child experiences difficulty at this stage the teacher ends the lesson and gives it again from the beginning on another day. These lessons also inform the teacher of defects in articulation. If the child cannot overcome these particular difficulties then they are attended to at some other time.

This particular way of teaching symbols is a phonic method. It is an attempt to secure a correct reproduction and a firm association with the movement necessary for tracing the symbol. The correct hearing of sounds is the first thing to be secured in any language, and if a language has a larger number of sounds than other languages, this correct hearing becomes more, not less, important.

This approach consists of using sandpaper letters. Other letters are divided into four trays with the first tray containing:

a e i o u m
d b y g n

When the teacher has taught one or two pairs of vowels she teaches a pair of consonants, e.g. d and b. When the two consonants have been mastered they are practised with the vowels already learnt—da, de, ba, be, taking care to give the correct short sound to the vowel. Later, the words dad, bad, bed, are dictated, analysed, composed and read with the child and so help him to distinguish the component sounds in words in which all the letters are sounded.

It is suggested that only a lesson on one pair of letters should be given at a time. The lesson is short, but after each new pair there is the need for plenty of tracing so that the forms of the letters learnt are thoroughly mastered.

The next stage is to take another pair of vowels, e.g. i and o. These are joined to the consonants already learned so that da, de, di, do, and ba, be, bi, bo can be sounded as the d and b are moved along in the tray next to the vowels. New words are now dictated—did, dob, bib, bob. The analysis, composition and re-reading give further initiation into the activity. But, not only must the tracing of the new letters be practised, but all the letters must be constantly traced.

Another pair of consonants is used, e.g. m and n. When these have been learnt they are joined on to vowels and form the series—ma, me, mi, na, ne, ni, no. More words are dictated for the child—mam, mad, man, min, ned, nin, nod. One more consonant, g, is eventually used with d or b. This gives the series—ga, ge, gi, go. Big and beg are dictated followed by such words as bag, gid, god.

U and y form the last pair of vowels and when learnt the series da, de, di, do, du, ba, be, bi, bo, bu, ma, me, mi, mo, mu, na, ne, ni, no, nu, ga, ge, gi, go, gu are used giving plenty of 'muscular exercises'.

The y is used with several words already composed, namely, Bobby, daddy, mammy, Neddy, ninny, noddy, giddy, and new words such as dummy and bunny.

This entails six very short lessons with an abundance of independent tracing and composing of words already dictated, and new words. These lessons contain a great deal of word composition. Words are dictated (many are well-known to the child so that when he reads them they convey an idea to him). In these exercises, the child analyses, perfects and fixes his own spoken language. They promote a clear utterance and lay a foundation for accurate spelling. Eventually, the child becomes independent of the dictation of the teacher for considerable periods, indulging in free composition between the times when she dictates words. When the child.has composed a word, he replaces the letters in the tray and this increases his familiarity with them.

If the teacher considers that the child is fully prepared to write but does not begin, she waits a week to see if he will begin spontaneously and then encourages him to write. The regularity of the writing is assisted by having double lines on the blackboard or paper. The distance between these double lines makes it possible to write letters of the same size as the sand-paper letters. It is also suggested that children need help with double lines because they prevent the writing from sloping away from the straight and help him in getting tall and short letters in the right proportion. Montessori did not believe in a compulsory acquisition of writing or reading below the age of six, but she suggested that with her techniques it is natural and relatively easy for a child to write at four, and write and read at five.

The second tray contains:

```
a  e  ı  o  u  w
k  p  y  r  l  j
```

Many simple words are made with r and the letters already learnt—red, rob, rag, run, rim, rib, rid. Similarly with l—log, lag, lug, lad, lid, leg. Because r occurs in many words after the consonants b, d, and g, and children often find difficulty both in pronouncing and analysing these double sounds, it is suggested that they should be taught by using vowels—dra, dre, dri, dro, dru, bra, bre, bri, bro, bru, gra, gre, gri, gro, gru. The following words can then be dictated: drag, drug, drab, brag, brim, bran, drum, grog, grub, grin.

Another combination which is often a source of spelling mistakes involves the letter l—bl, dl, gl, e.g. bubble, middle, giggle.

The consonants k and p are used and taught with sandpaper letters and practised in the vowel series—kid, keg, drink, sink. P is practised with l—plan, plod, plug, plum, plump are analysed together with two-syllabled words like pimple, ripple, dimple.

J and w are traced and learnt. When these letters have been practised in the vowel series, the following words are composed:

jap, jig, jog, jug, jingle, Jim
wag, wig, wind, wing, wink

J is associated with the second sound for g and a few words with 'ge' are taught—bridge, nudge, dodge, ledge, badge, judge.

Several words beginning with wr have an unsounded w and a few of these are made with the letters already known—wren, wring, wrong, wriggle. Similarly w with a silent h—whip, whim, when.

It is suggested that because children are inclined to mis-pronounce long vowels, it is advisable to teach these early.

The third tray contains the consonants with many variants standing for some of the sounds for which there are no letters in the alphabet (44 sounds). These are sounds which give rise to many spelling mistakes. This tray contains:

c s x z v
q t   h f

The forms and principal sounds of these consonants are taught with the sandpaper letters, a pair at a time—cab, sob, box, zoo, van, tap, hob, fan.

If children have not yet mastered the use of the aspirate, they need intensive lessons. Those vowels followed by single con-sonants, such as those in the first tray and some in the second

23

tray, are pronounced with and without the h:

ab, eb, ib, ob, ub
hab, heb, hib, hob, hub
ap, ep, ip, op, up,
hap, hep, hip, hop, hup

Each time a child composes a word with the movable letters he writes the word in his record book. The words are studied until he knows them thoroughly. Occasionally the teacher asks the child to read words from his record book or to write some of them on the blackboard. The size of the movable letters makes it possible for the teacher to know what words a large number of children are composing.

The fourth tray contains extra vowel sounds—ai, ay, oi, oy, ea, ow, ou, oa, ar, ur, er, ir etc.

Montessori found that many young children only appeared to be reading books. They were actually pronouncing the printed words but were not gathering the meaning. She originated the so-called 'commands' written on cards. She encouraged the children to read these commands silently and then carry out the actions indicated. Children picked reading slips from a basket, read them silently, and then performed the activity. Those children who could not read were helped by those who could. At a later stage, the children wrote their own commands and, as a result of observing the actions of other children, found out if they had expressed themselves clearly.

Nowhere is a reading primer used, and throughout there is opportunity for the child to express his own interests by frequent choice of words to be composed and written at the stage of mechanical writing, and by original commands, descriptions or poems at a later stage. There is a graduated series of passages for reading which the children interpret dramatically, thus showing that they have understood the precise meaning of the sentences and can reveal through gesture, attitude and facial expression what the author intended when he wrote the passage.

Methods—a few conclusions

My experience over the years in the teaching of reading has convinced me that there are many children failing to read because of their lack of phonic knowledge. Time and time again, I have noticed that even though children have acquired fairly large sight vocabularies and have continued to assist these sight vocabularies by 'guessing' new words through the use of contextual clues and illustrations, they inevitably encounter many words which are either not recognised by sight or are not read because there may not be contextual or pictorial clues to assist them. It is obviously essential that children have the necessary tools to 'unlock' such words.

I appreciate that many junior schools must be prepared to teach certain children the 'beginnings' of reading, but far too many of these schools have to concentrate on teaching too many of these children the basic letter sounds. Frequently, the 'look and say' method used in certain infant schools is too restrictive and does not provide a fundamental grounding in these basic sounds.

Too many 'educationists' have been advising teachers to allow their children to discover reading and not to force them along too quickly—'they will read when they are ready'. *Maybe the inclusion of phonics has been neglected because, with the growth of child-centred education, the theory was stressed that learning to read will best take place when motivation arising through interest is present and that children would be interested in words that are meaningful to them. Because some of these words might be rather long or phonically irregular, it was not possible in any case to teach them using a phonic method.*

It is unfortunate that controversy over the years about the best method of teaching reading has prevented many teachers from appreciating that _every method has its place_. For many years the phonic and 'look and say' methods have each claimed to possess the key to the best method of teaching reading. Many people have advocated one method to the absolute exclusion of the other. There have been charges and countercharges and heated arguments between the two schools of thought. Controlled experiments have been carried out from which conclusions about a method's relative values have been hoped for.

The questions have been: Should the child be taught the letter sounds of the alphabet first and then learn to sound out words letter by letter? Or should teaching begin with the pattern of a familiar word which the child will learn to recognise by its shape and configuration?

The many experiments have proved that the differing abilities of teachers to apply different methods have led to inconclusive and confusing results. Claims are frequently made for a particular method because improvement in reading has, on average and over a relatively short period, been greater when compared with the use of another method. However, when the children are tested after a follow-up investigation, there is frequently no significant difference between the effects of the two methods.

Probably the proponents of the 'look and say' method are correct in condemning a pure phonic method consisting of boring drill in order to teach the blending of separate sounds. This can have very little interest for the child. Probably the proponents of the phonic method are correct in condemning the 'look and say' method because *it* may involve too much mechanical drill. But there is no doubt that a child must learn by considerable repetition in order to associate the shape of a word with the name attached to it.

Today, however, more teachers are using 'mixed' methods, and more and more proponents of the 'look and say' method are recognising the value of meaningful phonic analysis, especially when it is applied, initially, to whole words, preferably words a child has already learned to recognise by sight.

I have found that when children first learn to read there is no need for 'formal' phonics because, if children are forced into using word analysis at this stage, their attention to letters will interfere with the ability to look for meaning in what is being read. The learning of sounds can be carried out in a more incidental manner. Children, generally, at the beginning stage of reading, learn to recognise words by their shapes or configurations.

I have obtained the best results by beginning with the 'look and say' method but introducing preparatory phonics at a very much earlier age than that suggested by many educationists. These preparatory phonics do not interfere with the child's ability to look for meaning in what he is reading because word analysis is not introduced at this stage. I do not rely exclusively on seeing and hearing but include touch and movement. It is very important that children have the opportunity of using finger tracing, sandpaper letters and writing in the sand tray, especially in the infant school, so that they have the 'feel' of letters and words.

My use of early phonics involves the occasional five minute period for phonic readiness activities and games. Many initial sounds may be taught in an incidental manner. Suggestions for preparatory phonic activities are found in *Aids to Reading* (by J. M. Hughes, Evans Brothers, 1970) and *Phonics and the*

Teaching of Reading (by J. M. Hughes, Evans Brothers, 1972). Eventually, as the children build up adequate sight vocabularies, the periods devoted to more 'formal' phonics become longer and more frequent, but the various sounds are taught using meaningful whole words. It is extremely important that phonic teaching is carefully graded, regular and systematic, and it must not be seen as reading when a child merely pronounces what the sounds say without realising the full meaning.

I dispute the contention of many investigators that children must have a certain mental age (usually six-and-a-half to seven-and-a-half) before a real start on reading can begin. I would agree with a growing body of opinion that the tasks involved can be accomplished by many children at surprisingly early ages. There has been a trend towards allowing children to read at a later age. There are children, however, of superior mental ability who are two or three years ahead of the average and who can, and should, read at a very much earlier age. The findings of Professor Bloom of the University of Chicago suggest that not only is intelligence a developing function, but that in terms of 'adult' intelligence measured at seventeen years, the child has developed 50 per cent by the time he is four, another 30 per cent between four and eight, and a final 20 per cent between eight and seventeen years. The five-year-old starts school during a period of comparatively rapid growth in mental ability. Of course intelligence has many facets, for example children may be slower in some areas of development of visual and auditory perception.

Sounds and phonic rules should be taught through the use of words and, whenever possible, words contained in a child's sight vocabulary and/or speech vocabulary. It must be remembered that meaningful reading should be the aim on all occasions and exercises must be provided so that children can apply newly acquired skills to new situations. When phonic teaching is based on a child's sight vocabulary and language experience, it means that he is taught to recognise whole words— for example, 'dog', before he is taught the sounds of the symbols 'd', 'o' and 'g'. At the beginning stage of reading, the word 'dog' is more meaningful than the three symbols from which it is formed.

The foundations of phonics are established once the child has acquired a number of sight words and the teacher brings the child's attention to the sounds associated with the initial letters of these known words. It is important that sounds are learned within the whole word because it is impossible to tell the sound of a certain letter, except for its pronunciation in the word in which it occurs. It is impossible to know that the letter 'a' out of context stands for the sound as in 'cat, ate, water, all, care, are, was' and 'about'. It is impossible to know that 's' out of context stands for the sound of 'z' as in 'is', 'sh' as in 'sure', 's' as in 'bus' or has no sound at all as in 'island'.

The ability to tackle unfamiliar words is a basic skill which must be acquired. A child will study the context and look for clues. He may recognise a word because of its pattern, length, final letter or letter groupings. This leads to guessing and there is a danger that this habit may lead to indiscriminate guessing. Even though children are able to recognise the pattern of many words, they must eventually have phonic knowledge in order to become accomplished readers. 'Look and say' on its own does not have the key to the unlocking of many unknown words; it does not help children to spell, and, unfortunately, too many children confuse words of similar configurations.

In order to tackle unfamiliar words, a child must be able to associate the sound of a letter or letters with the printed symbol or symbols. He must know the sound of individual letters, especially the initial letters of words. It is necessary for him to have knowledge of certain phonic combinations such as vowels and consonants—e.g. an, en, in, at, it; vowel digraphs—e.g. oo, ee, oa, ay; consonant digraphs—e.g. ch, sh, th, wh; consonant blends—e.g. st, sp, bl, tr. He must be able to analyse unfamiliar words and be able to recognise these phonic combinations and, above all, be able to recombine these sounds in order to build up a word.

It is unfortunate that many teachers are still suffering from the misconception that phonic teaching must consist of boring word-drill, and too many are unaware that phonic teaching can include other methods and approaches and many interesting discovery activities and games which are fully enjoyed by children. I have found that those children who have been given the opportunity to participate in preparatory phonic activities and training benefit immensely in that they become more confident and better equipped to help themselves in reading at a later stage.

Phonic analysis involves the ability to identify the sounds of the English language, the symbols devised to represent them and the ability to associate sound with symbol. *But* to equip a child with a knowledge of phonics and to ignore other skills and approaches involved in the teaching of reading will limit his fluency and efficiency in reading. Reading is more than translating symbols into speech. Surely, the ability to read means that one is able to get ideas and information from the printed page. Even though the development of independence in reading depends on the acquisition of methods of unlocking the pronunciation of words, it must be remembered that reading is a process of getting meaning from printed word symbols and is more than just a mechanical process and the making of noises associated with certain symbols.

A selection of reading materials and innovations

As a result of continued research in reading and related disciplines, combined with new insights into the interests of individual children, gradual changes are taking place in approach, materials and media. Educationists are continually searching for new methods of teaching reading, and new materials and aids for this teaching, but it must be remembered that the way they are used is the key to success. (A more comprehensive list of materials is provided in Appendix B.)

Breakthrough to Literacy
(Longman, for the Schools Council programme in linguistics and English teaching.)
Three practising teachers seconded to the Schools Council Initial Literacy Programme were convinced that:
  a the five-year-old can compose written language from the earliest stage
  b the production of language (writing) and reception (reading) go hand in hand
  c existing schemes impose on our children stilted and unnatural sentences that bear little relationship to the language that they themselves habitually use
  d traditional schemes inhabit a suburban, middle-class Never-Never-Land which is far away from either the environment or the fantasy world of most children.
  Breakthrough to Literacy presents a basic 'look and say' approach but it also takes account of approaches and methods which make the child aware of phonics. All the materials used were devised in the presence of children. The children involved

in the experiment included infants, juniors, ESN children, partially hearing children and some training school children.

The Literacy Programme is not merely a reading scheme, but a co-ordinated scheme in language—both reading and writing—arising from speaking and listening. The aim of the scheme is to develop the child's comprehension naturally out of the parents' habits of speech and reading, and to avoid any material and phrases foreign to the child's environment. The child is encouraged to value his own store of words and to supplement this from the linguistic materials developed from the project.

The materials in *Breakthrough to Literacy* consist of 'My Sentence Maker' which is regarded as the basic tool for each child. There is a larger version for the teacher. There are twenty-four 'Breakthrough Books' for supplementary reading and two 'Big Breakthrough Books': *About the house* and *An ABC for happy girls and boys*. These two books are used to introduce the alphabet to the children in a humorous and interesting way.

There is a record containing fifty-two nursery rhymes. The children are able to listen to the nursery rhymes and read the words on 'Nursery Rhyme Cards'. The Magnet Pack consists of a Magnet Board, magnets and brightly coloured cut-out figures. This Magnet Board is an improved version of the Flannelgraph and holds both words and pictures which give rise to factual and imaginative discussion. A Teacher's Manual gives practical suggestions for the use of all the materials.

The Sentence Maker may be regarded as the basic tool for language work and the folder holds a set of 130 printed word cards. These will include many of the words that a child will need. There are blank cards available for any additional words required. The child is introduced to his own Sentence Maker when he is able to recognise certain words through handling the teacher's large replica of the·Sentence Maker. The child selects words from his folder as he needs them and constructs sentences by arranging the words in the correct order. If a child wants a word which cannot be found, then the teacher writes it on a blank card. When the children have constructed sentences in the plastic stands provided for them, the teacher prints them in the children's books. These become the children's first reading books.

The variety of reading material enables children to come in contact with many forms of language. When children are proficient in making their own sentences, they use the Word Maker.

The Word Maker helps children to appreciate the ways in which words are made. The apparatus consists of a folder containing letters and letter combinations printed on cards, e.g. th, wh, sh and ch. Children use the Word Maker to attempt the spelling of new words and to play spelling games. The basic 'look and say' approach used by means of the Sentence Maker gradually merges with phonics as a result of using the Word Maker. This enables children to construct words experimentally, without the finality of writing. The twenty-four reading books contain the same kinds of sentences which the children have been constructing in their plastic stands.

All aspects of language development are incorporated into the scheme and the materials centre around the individual interests of each child.

The SRA Reading Laboratories

The SRA Reading Laboratories are intended as a reading aid and not to replace other reading schemes. They allow the teacher more time to help those in most need and act as a challenge to good readers.

The reading laboratories are designed to meet the needs of children of varying ranges of ability in a given age group. The reading material is graded very carefully from a basic elementary level to adult level. The aim of the laboratories is to improve comprehension, vocabulary and speed. Because not all children of the same age will reach the stage of being able to read at the same time, the Reading Laboratory Series gives each child a course that is geared to his own ability level, and skills are acquired at the child's own rate of learning. The laboratories cater for children in infant and junior schools who are still learning the basic decoding process.

Initial motivation is based on a series of interesting and colourful stories. Because the laboratories were originally designed for the requirements of American schools, the stories contain many Americanisms. But these Americanisms do not appear to affect adversely the child's enjoyment of the material.

The child works his way through a laboratory, marking and scoring his own work. The various levels within each laboratory are colour-coded. The child scores and corrects his reading exercises and records the results on his own progress card.

The first Reading Laboratories are 1 (Word Games), 1a, 1b and 1c. The children are introduced to the work contained in these laboratories by means of a Listening Skill Builder. The teacher reads stories aloud from the Teacher's Handbook and then asks questions. The children select their answers from a group given in their record books. They can check their answers and record their scores on progress charts in 'My Own Book for Listening'.

Reading Laboratory 1: Word Games contains forty-four games and these cover 136 phonic and structural analysis skills. The children play individually or in pairs and play those games listed on their programmes.

The Power Builders help to build comprehension and test vocabulary and word attack at all levels. They contain brightly illustrated, informative stories. The children record their times, answer questions, check their answers and record their results.

The Rate Builders start with Laboratory 2a. These are shorter, three-minute reading exercises. Here the teacher signals the start and finish. Each exercise is followed by questions and the children correct their answers.

Science Research Associates have published BRS Satellites, (this is a library for beginning readers) and SRA Pilot Libraries. (Each library contains seventy-two Pilot Books.)

The Programmed Reading Kit (Holmes McDougall)

The kit is a set of materials designed to impart phonic skills. The material is arranged into individual and group games which are largely self-corrective. This is an attempt to break away from the classic stereotypes of alternative methods. The kit consists of a series of thirty teaching aids and is sufficient for a group of four or six children, or more if they are at different stages, or progress at different rates.

Children use the material for playing games. Learning is self-corrective resulting in the child teaching himself or a group of children teaching each other. Progress Cards are provided and as the child masters each item, he colours in a corresponding section on his Progress Card.

Dr D. H. Stott has tried to devise a kit which ensures that the learning processes involved are finely programmed so that the child may move on quite easily from one stage to the next. The kit is so designed that a class at very different stages may be kept productively occupied without needing constant attention. Thus the kit's self-learning features have a very important attribute. Stott suggests that a child should not be taught the sounds of individual letters, but allowed to learn them incidentally. The letter/sound associations are mastered naturally, and are acquired in an almost unconscious manner. This is done by allowing the child to learn them incidentally as a result of associating the names of objects with their illustrations.

This kit is extremely useful because it may be used as supplementary material with any reading scheme or with any other approach.

The tape recorder

When one considers the normal classroom situation, one quickly appreciates that a child must be left for some time before the results of his reading efforts can be checked by the teacher. An approach can be adopted, however, whereby the teacher ensures that she is able to give individual attention to one child and yet know that the other children are actively engaged and are learning. A teaching programme can be devised whereby children are involved in a reading situation and assisted in their reading, *almost* as if they were being taught on a one-to-one basis.

Taped reading lessons can be prepared and headphones can be plugged into the output extension of the tape recorder (The Primary Audio Set, S. G. Brown Ltd., King George's Avenue, Watford, Herts). Many suggestions have been put forward for using the tape recorder as a teaching aid for reading and these can be found in the works of Jones (1962), Weston (1968), Hughes (1969), (1970) and (1971).

The Clifton Audio/Visual Reading Programme is basically a phonic approach using taped material, reading cards and workbooks. The Remedial Supply Company supplies an abundance of taped reading material. *The Ladybird Key Words Reading Scheme* is now available in taped-lesson form for the first six reading books ('a' series). Music is used to promote good modulation and rhythm. Tapes and cassettes are available.

I have found that when children first use the tape recorder and headphones as a reading aid the novelty effect of the machine is highly motivating. But even when the novelty has worn off, the motivation remains.

The tape recorder is valuable as a reading aid for the following reasons:

   a If the lessons are carefully graded, there is none of the
     anxiety which a slow reader experiences in trying to

33

    struggle through a book in the normal classroom situation.

b This is a highly motivating method of introducing children to reading.

c It produces success for children who are accustomed to failure.

d The approach promotes listening. This is an important aspect in helping children to reach a true state of readiness for 'beginning' reading. This is frequently difficult to provide in a normal classroom.

e Since the child should have already listened to the story during the first recorded reading, he can apply himself more to the content because he has already formed a picture of the sequence of events in the story.

f Since most reading depends on the memorising of word patterns, this approach gives children additional practice in increasing their acquaintance with a simple vocabulary.

g It provides an opportunity for the individualisation of work in skill building by providing uninterrupted learning of reading skills with as many repetitions as the child requires.

h The child becomes more confident when asked to read to his teacher or anyone else.

i It provides an excellent means of helping the child who misses important work because of occasional absences.

The inconsistencies of English spelling

Because the English language contains many inconsistencies, attempts have been made to overcome the fact that the correlation between sounds and symbols does not have a consistent one-to-one relationship. Many educationists, appreciating that English spelling is frequently inadequate and ambiguous, have looked for new approaches which will give children more phonetic assistance. Diacritical marks have been used to indicate that a vowel may either make the sound of its name—for example, gāte, wīne, rōse, or make a shorter sound—căt, sĭt, pŏt. Sir James Pitman's i.t.a. is yet another attempt to overcome the inconsistencies of the English language.

Colour has been used as an aid to the recognition of the sound value of letters by several educationists including Moxon (1962),

Gattegno (1962), E. and W. Bleasdale (1966), Jones (1967) and Mosely (1971). The first book to be printed entirely in colour was published in 1899. Nellie Dale brought out a series of books using three colours plus black. Black for voiced consonants, blue for unvoiced consonants, red for vowels and yellow for silent letters.

Colour Story Reading (Nelson & Sons Ltd.)

J. K. Jones based his *Colour Story Reading* (1965) on the results of tests involving discrimination of words, shapes and letters. These tests showed that children obtained far higher scores when tested with material in colour than when tested with similar material in black print.

Colour Story Reading was designed to give complete consistency and reliability to the phonetic clues in black print by using three colours, red, blue and green plus black. There is no change in the shape of letters and traditional spelling is retained.

Reading books are used and colour is used in the following examples to show how Jones keeps traditional letters consistent and reliable:

a 'Do', 'shoe', 'too', 'true', 'two' and 'through' all end with the same sound but all have different spellings.

b 'county', 'cough', 'course', and country' all begin with the same three letters but are all pronounced in different ways.

Jones uses nine coloured backgrounds representing sounds, except for the blue circle which represents 'silence'. Letters are printed in black on either three blue backgrounds, three red or three green and each background is either square, or triangular or circular. It is suggested that the colour symbol code should be regarded as a temporary prop and should be dropped once the child is reading fluently. It is also suggested that even though *Colour Story Reading* is phonetic, the initial approach should be by 'look and say', 'whole word' or sentence methods.

The colour symbol code is displayed on a wallchart and contains fifty-three colour symbols representing forty-two sounds and silent letters. Letters which cannot be coded are printed in black and many of these black letters are regular.

Words in Colour (Cuisenaire Co. Ltd.)

Words in Colour was devised by Dr Gattegno. He analysed the English language into its constituent sounds and represents each sound by a colour. He maintains conventional spelling.

The differing ways in which a sound is represented in English spelling is portrayed on Fidel Charts and over forty colours are used. These colours are on twenty-one wallcharts which are used for teaching groups of children or the whole class. In the initial stages, the materials consist of coloured chalks, a wooden pointer and the wallcharts. Letters on these wallcharts are coloured consistently according to the sound which they represent in certain words. A form of phonic drill is used and the teacher taps letters with the pointer asking the children what the sounds are. For example, 'a' as in 'mat' is chanted—a,aaa, a,aaa,aaa. Consonants are given no sounds of their own, but are only shown to sound with vowels. They are taught in the same way once the five vowels have been taught. Consonants and vowels are eventually blended until the child reads such sentences as 'pat stops spot' and 'pup trips pat'.

Gattegno maintains that, with no help from the teacher, the children are free to use their own powers using shape, colour, position on the chart, or a key word, as guides to sounds with no complete reliance on any one of these factors because, in practice, writing and reading develop step by step.

The Initial Teaching Alphabet (i.t.a.)

i.t.a. consists of forty-four characters. Twenty-four letters from our existing alphabet are retained and twenty new symbols are added. i.t.a. must be regarded as a medium and *not* a method. It is suggested that teachers should use the methods they are accustomed to.

Some of the main features of i.t.a. are:

a It has only one print configuration for each English word, e.g. 'cat' and not Cat or CAT, etc.

b It usually has only one symbol for each sound unit or phoneme. For example, ⍵ is used for a variety of symbols for this sound in traditional orthography (t.o.): blue, too, shoe, zoo, through, fruit, etc.

c It removes the irregularity of the relations between sound and printed symbols, e.g. 'o' as in one, bone, gone, etc., and 'a' as in was, water, mat, hare, cake, about, etc. This is replaced by a coding which represents these different vowel sounds.

d Where the two parts of the letter group are separated by another letter, this sound is represented by a single character, e.g. fine—fien, hive—hiev, ride—ried.

e It is designed to ease transition on t.o. As far as possible the upper part of the i.t.a. configuration of whole words is similar to the upper part of t.o. configuration.

There has been much controversy over the use and value of i.t.a. and there is an abundance of literature on the subject including that of Downing (1966), Southgate (1965 and 1967) and the Inner London Education Authority (1963–67). Warburton and Southgate (1969) carried out an independent evaluation of i.t.a. for the Schools Council. The evidence, collected from a variety of sources, comes out in favour of the use of i.t.a. Research indicated that in most schools, *but not all,* infants using i.t.a. have learnt to read earlier and faster than similar children using t.o. However, evidence suggests that after nearly three years of using i.t.a. the reading ability of the 't.o.' children is at the same level as those who began with i.t.a. Teachers using i.t.a. found that their children had no difficulty in transferting to t.o. Researchers, however, found that some children experience a setback in reading attainment after transition.

The evidence of the independent evaluation suggested a need for more research into the early stages of learning to read and into methods of assessing reading ability.

Chapter 3

The initial stages of reading

Language development

It is necessary to provide many young children with a wide range of pre-reading activities. All these activities help to enrich the children's experiences, foster the growth of language and encourage awareness, concentration and attention. These many activities involve the use of water, clay, sand, puppets, imaginative play, etc. The various forms of children's play help the children to discover, experience and interpret. It is from the natural activities of everyday work and play that language is encouraged through writing, drawing, painting, reading, acting and talking about things and events. The part that language plays in the formation of concepts is of vital importance. 'Without the use of language the genetical potential of intelligence cannot be fully exploited' (McNally and Murray, 1962.)

When the child relates words to illustrations of things and events, he begins labelling and naming. This helps the child to classify his many experiences. He categorises, compares, discriminates and sorts. But it must be remembered that all children need time to develop various forms of classification and, in particular, need time to develop the fine discriminations between symbols and sound patterns. Gradually the child becomes more perceptive and aware of relationships.

Speech and reading are so closely related that they must not be regarded as isolated skills because, after all, reading involves the ability to use the spoken word together with the ability to recognise print, and then translate it by relating it to one's experience and knowledge. As a child tends to interpret the spoken word through gestures and facial expressions, reading can be more difficult because the recognition of visual symbols has to be carried out without these aids.

A language development programme

Children with adequate intellectual and cultural backgrounds acquire efficiency in language informally and often incidentally, but children from culturally deprived backgrounds and the intellectually slow are not so fortunate. More and more educationists are appreciating that better systematic procedures need to be developed for measuring and stimulating growth of the psycholinguistic processes of children with potential learning handicaps. The *Illinois Test of Psycholinguistic Abilities* (Kirk and McCarthy, 1961) is designed to measure these processes.

The language development programme can be designed to serve all children and it stresses the training of a global oral language approach with emphasis on reception, expression and conceptualisation. There are kits on the market for such training including the *Peabody Language Development Kits* (American Guidance Service, 1965). However, this kit is expensive and would not be used in many schools. We can, however, follow certain guide lines when planning a language development programme.

  a The teacher should ensure that language lessons are games and there should be more time for talk and activity than is usually allowed.
  b A language development programme is not intended to replace the regular activities in everyday use in the classroom but rather to supplement them.
  c The teacher should ensure that the activities are pupil-centred. There should be an atmosphere allowing for more spontaneity in speech than during the normal lesson. Language development is a talking time for the children and the teacher's role is not so much to do the talking but to involve the children.
  d The children should be given an opportunity to repeat activities successfully. The activities should be varied in order to sustain a high level of interest.

Language programme activities may include the following:

  a Naming as many groups of objects and animals as possible in five minutes by asking such questions as: What do we use to dig a hole, cut a cake, sweep a path, peel an apple, etc.?
  b Listening activities such as: Sounds of animals, clapping out a tune, etc.

39

c Classification exercises, e.g.: What do we call animals that fly? What do we call all the things that we wear?
d Conversation exercises: Ask the children to describe their likes and dislikes. Ask them to complete sentences.
e Following instructions.

Pictures and words

This is a language and reading development scheme devised by Dr Elizabeth Goodacre and published by Blackie & Son Ltd. The scheme consists of two large (47 cm by 59 cm) Teacher's Display Books, each containing six pictures; twelve Pupils' Books, each of which takes the title of one of the display pictures and deals with particular sections of it; a detailed Teacher's Guide which explains how all the material can be used.

The large pictures depict incidents and environments found in many of the popular reading schemes. Words likely to be encountered in such schemes or needed in free writing are imposed on the large pictures. The large pictures are used as discussion material and to provide children with the experience of recognising familiar objects or actions. A number of the objects identified in the large pictures are available as toys or models, and children can be encouraged to handle either scaled-down versions or construct their own models. This helps the children to grasp the basic concept that a word stands for something, and gradually word labels can replace the named object. The material and approach help the teacher to ascertain the extent of a child's grasp of the technical vocabulary of learning to read, i.e. the use of the terms and language concepts, *word, letter, sound, beginning, end, middle, shape,* etc.

The Pupils' Books contain several different types of printed material—sections of the large picture, outline figures, black and white line drawings of objects or actions, words in lower case lettering. The small books can be used as pre-reading material, or as a checking device to assess the child's progress in attaining pre-reading skills of concept formation and visual and auditory discrimination. These exercises can form a basis for the introduction of phonics, because the teacher can observe the child's ability to understand the meaningful use of symbols: to recognise differences between words, to discriminate between spoken words; to recognise word beginnings including

40

consonants, consonant blends, consonant digraphs, consonants with more than one sound, and silent letters.

The scheme is systematic but flexible enough for teachers to adapt it or use it as supplementary material.

SRA Language Development Programme

The SRA Language Development Kit consists of ninety-six Language Builder Story Boards divided into topic units. Seventy-seven of these Boards show colour photography and nineteen show black and white photographs (145 cm by 43 cm). The kit contains a graded list of recommended books for project work based on the topics discussed with the use of the Story Boards. A Teacher's Guidebook provides an abundance of suggestions, including discussion questions for each panel of each Story Board, and language activities arising from the children's dialogues. Each panel is part of a whole story. There is a pad of dialogue paper, a marker pen and adhesive putty. The carefully planned box of pictures may be used throughout the school.

The Language Development Programme is designed for use with a whole range of children: the very young who are still developing language patterns, those of limited cultural background, and those who use very little spoken English and need considerable language development. The Language Builder Story Boards are open-ended to encourage the children to involve themselves in a variety of interpretations and to grasp the concept being shown by means of language. Group discussion is used so that children develop their own story and dialogue according to their particular interests and language needs. This language is written on dialogue paper and adhesive putty is used to attach it to a panel. Here an attempt is made to provide a visual introduction to the function of reading. The teacher uses the Story Boards to encourage the children to talk about familiar family and community situations.

Classroom activities

It is important that, before a child learns to read, he fully appreciates that ideas are found from the black marks on paper. The black marks on the front of a bus tell him where the bus is going; the black marks under a picture tell him what is happening in the picture, and the first series of black marks on the envelope containing his birthday card actually represent his name. The teacher should use every opportunity to provide activities that involve the association of the written word with day-to-day happenings in the classroom. A tremendous amount of preparatory reading work takes place as the children express their own ideas verbally; begin to interpret illustrations; record their thoughts and ideas in the form of drawing, painting, building, clay-modelling and acting; enjoy stories associated with pictures and stories being read to them by the teacher; re-tell these stories to the teacher or other children in the class; practise, quite incidentally, many perceptual abilities such as form perception, hand/eye co-ordination, visual copying, visual memory, visual rhythm, visual sequencing, visual discrimination, auditory memory and discrimination.

All activities and experiences provided should be such that they encourage the child to want to read. During the stage of reading preparation, the child should have experiences which will help to develop his powers of visual and auditory discrimination, his level of spoken vocabulary, listening, and social and emotional maturity.

Children learn to speak as a result of being in an environment where speech is part of everyday life, and when they begin school they should enter an environment where the written word is also part of everyday living. Children should be in a classroom environment where they are able to express their own ideas in as many ways as possible. The classroom should provide colourful books of all kinds, covering a wide range of interests. Children should be encouraged to handle books, look at pictures and talk about what they see. The convention of opening books at the beginning, turning over in the correct manner and following lines of print from left to right begins here.

The teacher reads stories, talks about pictures and encourages the children to talk about them. Children should be surrounded by colourful and interesting displays and various objects carrying labels, phrases and sentences. It is at this stage that the teacher provides opportunities for relating experiences and happenings with the written word. Various charts and notices will inform children of their various tasks and activities, as in the following example:

Mary	Weather chart and calendar
John	Sharpen the pencils
June and Jane	Give out the milk
Brian	Feed the hamster
Jean	Water the flowers
George and Wayne	Wash the paintbrushes
Ann	Give out the drawing paper
Elizabeth	Give out the clay

It is very important to remember that notices should be removed when they have served their purpose. If they are left on the walls too long, the children will ignore them because they become lost in the many pictures, charts, lists, etc.

The making of books is a very important activity in learning to read. Such books are made from the child's own ideas, words and sentences. The teacher encourages the child to talk and write about as many interests and activities as possible so that he builds up a vocabulary of words which are meaningful and interesting. Many children are discouraged at the initial stages of reading if they encounter too many difficulties with published reading books. Teacher-made, child-made and children-made books have a very important role to play at this stage. The teacher may write a book with the children's help. Children may select a topic or theme which they find interesting. After discussing the topic with the children, the teacher may write a few sentences about the topic. The early pages should contain simple sentences beginning with three, four or five words. The teacher may gradually increase the length and number of sentences as the book is gradually built up. The teacher may find that she has to encourage the child to trace over the words with his finger or with a pencil/crayon, and to say the words as he traces them. The teacher decides when the child can dispense with the tracing. When this approach is adopted, the teacher helps the child to build up a 'sight vocabulary'. She may eventually allow the child to 'overwrite' her own writing when he has drawn his own pictures. Such a book can be built up page by page and contain those words used by the child in everyday speech. These books may be prepared for individual children and for small groups.

It is during this period that the teacher will be observing her children and noting if they are:

a developing favourable work attitudes

b showing persistence

c   exhibiting powers of sustained attention
d   able to recognise similarities and differences
e   aware of spatial relationships when using jigsaws
f   showing an interest in books and a desire to read
g   listening with attention to a story being read
h   able to carry out verbal instructions
i   exhibiting normal vision, hearing and motor control
j   physically normal and do not tire easily

Before or during the time children begin to read their first readers, it is suggested that they become accustomed to the words contained in them. Many first readers have much supplementary material which will help to provide the necessary extra practice. Often teachers use published material which involves the matching of words and pictures, simple sentences and pictures. Much of this material involves various useful discriminative skills particularly important for the slower child. But it should be remembered that the best apparatus and material are made by the teacher to help overcome specific difficulties experienced by individuals or small groups of children. Preparation for reading involves many pre-reading activities. These activities may not be required for all children but the teacher should ensure that all children have mastered certain skills. Some children find it difficult to listen for any period of time, so the reading of stories to children should be used to encourage the essential habit of listening.

The teacher should study the various games and activities available, analyse the skills which they promote and the level of difficulty which they represent. A game or activity indulged in for too long a period without substitution of new ideas can lead to 'overlearning' of something known very well already. If the game or activity is such that a child can add new items and thus use various adaptations, the value of the material is further extended. The following are points which the teacher should have in mind when deciding on the various reading games which she wishes to use:

a   Do they provide exercises for the development of preparation for reading?
b   Do they place the onus of active learning on the child?
c   Do they help to establish word recognition?
d   Do they help in diagnosing a child's difficulties?
e   Do they involve listening, speaking and writing activities?

f   Is learning carefully graded?

g   Are the various skills being taught rather than being tested?

h   Do they provide opportunities for self-evaluation?

i   Are the instructions simple and clear enough for the child to involve himself in the activity?

j   Do they provide opportunities for silent as well as oral participation?

The reading programme

Learning to read is related to other aspects of a child's overall development, i.e. physical, social, intellectual and emotional aspects. Developments in these areas are continuous and may be accelerated at various stages. They are sequential and the different aspects of each development are interrelated. Therefore the ability to read is continuous and sequential, starting with pre-school experiences and then moving on to such skills as word recognition, and phonic analysis and synthesis. The teacher must identify the various sub-skills (Roberts, 1969), those sub-skills which are necessary for efficient reading and, at the same time, devise situations to ensure that the child has the opportunity of acquiring these sub-skills. It is also apparent that a teacher must have knowledge of diagnostic procedures which will help him to decide what reading programme is necessary for the child. It is necessary for the teacher to be able to select the appropriate material for a specific purpose and, at the same time, appreciate that she must be prepared to have at her disposal a variety of flexible reading materials and approaches. In order to do this, the teacher should have the knowledge and ability to appreciate the value of a wide range of reading materials and approaches.

A general outline
Let us consider a general outline for a programme which a teacher requires if she is to plan a developmental scheme leading on from the basic and incidental work which is continuously being carried out in the classroom:

a   The development of language
b   Motor skills

c   Visual skills
d   Auditory skills
e   Sight vocabulary
f   Comprehension skills
g   Word recognition skills
h   Phonic skills
i   Speed and fluency skills

During the preparatory period of learning to read a useful activity is the matching of three-dimensional models, followed by the matching of three-dimensional models to pictures. Provide the child with four pictures, e.g. car, bus, aeroplane and house. Ask the child to match models of these four objects with the pictures by placing the appropriate model on top of the picture.

Provide the child with a workbook containing pictures of common objects—four on each page. Ask the child to pick out one of the objects and colour it with the colour decided by the teacher as follows:

'Where is the car?'
'Colour it red.'

This exercise informs the teacher whether the child can select an object from three others and whether he knows a particular colour. Another exercise is to provide the child with a book containing many coloured objects. The teacher gives the child a series of clues such as:

'It is red.'
'It has four wheels.'
'We ride in it.'

The child should pick out the red bus. Several exercises of this kind will help the child develop a functional vocabulary. The teacher should use those words which the child will encounter in his first reader and those used in everyday conversation. At this stage many other language development activities may be used including those already discussed under 'Language Development'.

A basic sight vocabulary consists of a number of words found frequently in the speech, reading and writing of children. These 'sight words' are recognised without pictorial or contextual clues or phonic analysis. Many of these sight words cannot be illustrated and many are fairly short and similar in configuration. They are such important words that children should memorise them as early as possible during the initial stages of reading. If a child can instantly recognise these words this will greatly assist his reading progress because these words of common usage include 'as, and, are, have, his, in, of, the, they', etc.

An important pre-reading activity is another form of matching. Matching materials are provided with several reading schemes and they include picture/word matching cards. These deal with words the child will encounter in his first reading primer, or they may be 'key' words and will be used in much of the child's written work. These picture/word matching exercises can start by being quite simple but can be so programmed that they quickly become more complex. Another exercise involving the linkage of words and pictures is similar to bingo. This exercise can contain an element of competition because each child can be given a slightly different card so that the winner becomes the child who completes his card first. This bingo game may be played in various ways. The first may be based on a picture having a word linked to it by writing it underneath the picture. Eventually the pictures may be removed and the game is played with words only.

Useful materials at this stage:

From Galt & Co. Ltd.
Key Words Self Teaching Cards
Basic Words Lotto
Key Words Lotto

From Philip & Tacey Ltd.
Groundwork Key Words Coloured Gummed Stamps
Renown Individual Picture and Word Matching Cards

Throughout these exercises and games, together with the many other incidental activities involved in day-to-day activities of the classroom, there will be incidental introduction to letter sounds. The teacher should take every opportunity to show her pupils how letters and letter sounds appear time and time again in certain words.

Print the word

f _ _   h _ _ _ _ _

g _ _ _ _   v _ _ _   b _ _

d _ _ _   c _ _   c _ _ _ _

van   girl   house   fox
door   chair   cap   bag

Picture/word jigsaws
Select several sight words which you wish to teach and which can be illustrated. These pictures may be obtained from magazines and pasted on thin cardboard. Print the word under each picture and then cut the cards into two-piece jigsaws. Ensure that each card has a different cut from the others.

Read-the-word-board

This activity involves picture/word and word/word matching exercises using jigsaws. Collect illustrations with names which the teacher wishes to introduce. If these illustrations are not to be found in magazines, etc., simple line drawings may be used. Cut around each drawing. Print the word on each drawing. Cut

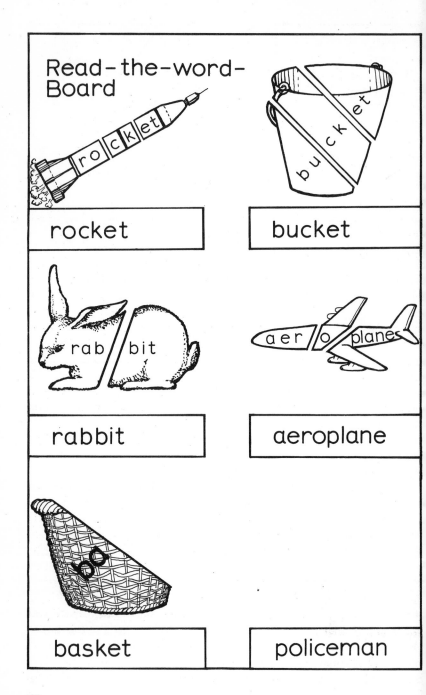

Read-the-word-Board

rocket

bucket

rabbit

aeroplane

basket

policeman

the drawing into two, three or four sections but do this in such a way that the constituent sound combinations of each word are separated. Place each jigsaw in a separate box or envelope.

The child should be shown how he will be able to read the word on the board if the jigsaw is put together correctly. The illustration will tell the child the word printed on it. This word must be found on the board and the illustration matched with it. The completed jigsaw is placed above the word on the board and the word is read aloud.

The read-the-word-board should be a piece of thin cardboard. Slits may be made in this cardboard so that the word may be held in place.

Children will eventually reach a stage when they will have acquired quite a substantial number of words learned by sight and some will already be constructing simple sentences. Already children are using visual and auditory discrimination of letters and letter sounds. Throughout this period, many children will be learning new words and simple sentences through drawing and adding the necessary captions. This activity will have been in progress for some time. A typical infants' class will contain many books or folders with colourful drawings and words and sentences. This is the basic framework on which much of the child's reading will be built and the majority of children will move along the 'reading road' fairly quickly. Those children experiencing difficulty will spend a longer period on the many exercises, games and activities mentioned above. The sight vocabulary of the better readers will be further extended through the use of the various word games and activities as suggested in *Aids to Reading* by J. M. Hughes (Evans Brothers).

The incidental introduction to sounds may be further extended by using word building apparatus with those children who are able to benefit. The usual procedure is to use a word already known by sight. The word 'dog' learned as a sight word is used in such a way that the child appreciates how the word can be built up and how the three sounds 'd', 'o' and 'g' can be blended together to form the word. At this stage the child is involved in more sound discrimination exercises. Some children experiencing difficulty at this stage will require more games and activities as suggested in *Phonics and the Teaching of Reading* by J. M. Hughes (Evans Brothers), and others will require more exercises in preparation for phonics. Frequently, at this stage, a sand tray may be used so that the child writes the word in the sand with the help of the teacher who may guide his finger; or sandpaper letters may be used so that the child gets the 'feel' of letters and words.

The teacher continues to concentrate on the teaching of 'key' sight words or simple sentence construction for those still experiencing difficulties in this area. 'Here is ......,' 'I see ......,' etc. are used very frequently in everyday speech and they make up a large percentage of written work. The following exercises may be useful at this stage:

Here is a _____

Here is the _____

This is a _____

This is the _____

I see a _____

I see the _____

bird	pig	box
cow	dog	bus

Using key sentences

This is a useful activity for those children who are beginning to read phrases and sentences. Provide two large envelopes for two separate sets of cards. One set should consist of phrase cards containing those words being used in the early stages of learning to read. The second set should consist of pictures and words. The children are encouraged to make sentences from the phrase cards and picture cards. The pictures may be obtained from magazines, etc.

Building a sight vocabulary : key word activities

The following nine stages provide an example of key word activities involving picture/word matching, word/word matching, picture/sentence matching, building key sentences, colours, colours and sentences, reading and colouring, and underlining the correct sentences.

Stage One involves the use of pictures and words. The child is asked to find a word to match the word on the picture. The teacher should print each word on the reverse side of the picture in preparation for Stage Two.

Stage Two involves the child in an activity which helps him to read the word without the use of a pictorial clue. He is allowed to turn the card over to check his response.

Stage Three involves word/word matching. Here the child is asked to match the words and read them.

Stage Four involves picture/sentence matching. Here the child is asked to select a sentence and match it with the sentence on the card.

Stage Five involves building key sentences. Here additional key sentences are introduced and the child is asked to read each sentence and place as many as possible on the appropriate cards.

Stage Six involves the use of colours. The child is asked to use the colour printed on each card.

Stage Seven is a further activity involving colouring and then the placing of correct sentences on the appropriate cards.

Stage Eight involves a revision activity. Here the child is asked to follow the instructions on the cards and then place these cards in their correct positions on the drawing. Writing exercises may be devised for this exercise as follows:

Put in the word :

> Here is a . . . . . . door
> I can see a . . . . . . house
> Look at the . . . . . . tree
> I like the . . . . . . dog
> This is my . . . . . . ball
> We can see a . . . . . . bird

Stage Nine involves the underlining of correct sentences.

stage one (picture/word matching)
words on reverse.

tree	bird	ball	cat

tree	bird	ball	cat

house	girl	dog	boy

house girl boy

stage two (reverse side of cards)

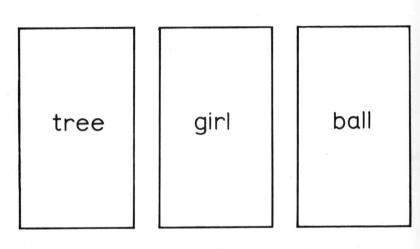

tree	girl	ball

stage three (word/word matching)

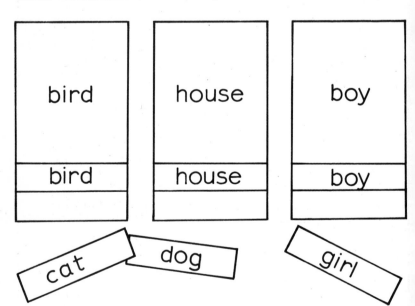

bird	house	boy
bird	house	boy

cat   dog   girl

stage four (picture/sentence matching)

Here is the tree

Here is the bird

Here is the bird

Here is the house

Here is the cat

Here is the tree

Here is the cat

Here is the house

stage five (building key sentences)

Here is the dog

I see the dog

I like the dog

Here is the boy

Look at the boy

I see the boy

This is a dog

I like the boy

Look at the dog

This is a boy

stage six (colours)

Colour the black dog	Colour the red house	Colour the green tree

stage seven (colours and sentences)

Colour the blue ball

Colour the brown cat

Colour the yellow bird

Here is a brown cat

I see a yellow bird

I like the black dog

I have a blue ball

Look at the green tree

We see a red house

stage eight (read and colour)

Here is a black chimney

I see a blue bird

chimney

This is a red roof

roof

window

door

Look at the green door

We like the black dog

Look at my black cat

This is my brown ball

Here is a red house

Look at the green tree

stage nine (underlining correct sentences)

	This is a tree This is the dog This is a bird
	We can see a ball We can see a door We can see a house
	Look at the big ball Look at the big door Look at the big bird
	Here is the house Here is the chimney Here is the door
	I like this white cat I like this white bird I like this white door
	I have a bird in my garden I have a tree in my garden I have a ball in my garden
	This is my cat This is my house This is my dog

During the initial stages of reading, the aim should be to bring the child from the learning of simple nouns to the use of these nouns in simple contexts. At the same time, the aim is to help the child learn those key words that cannot be illustrated but are so essential to reading, writing and understanding simple sentences, especially when these key words are used in different contexts—words such as 'here', 'they', 'there', 'are', etc. Simple sounds are still being learned incidentally but certain children move on to the learning of sound combinations, the blending of other sounds and eventually the learning of common digraphs.

When the child is ready, he starts to read simple books and will eventually experience a significant increase in the number of new words and, at a later stage, will move from simple phonic blending to more complex blending involving vowel and consonant digraphs. The mastery of this phonic stage will also assist the child's spelling. Some children may require considerable practice at this stage and various phonic games and activities should be used.

Different children will be adopting different methods of word attack. This may involve the memorising of common words either by remembering word patterns or by identifying certain features found within the whole pattern. The child may remember the word because of its length or its initial letter; groups of letters within the word may be the necessary cue, or the word may be read because of contextual or pictorial clues. Many children adopt their own form of word attack. They find suitable cues and respond accordingly. These children read fluently and are able to 'anticipate' words, language structure and comprehension.

But many children require the teacher's assistance in 'unlocking' words by using some form of phonic method. The necessary techniques will include appreciating rhymes; letter sound association; the use of initial letter sound and context in order to attack and read new words; constructing words from word parts; the ability to analyse words, i.e. to break up into constituent sounds, and the ability to synthesise, i.e. to blend these sounds to make the whole word.

Useful books at this stage are:
Gay Way Red Stories (Macmillan)
Sounds and Words Stories (ULP)
Moving on with Reading (Nelson)

Preparation for phonics

The teacher should teach sounds and phonic rules through the use of words, and, whenever possible, words contained in a child's sight vocabulary and/or speech vocabulary. It should be remembered that meaningful reading should be the aim at all times and exercises and activities should be provided in such a way that the child is able to apply newly acquired skills to new situations.

The better readers will probably have an understanding of phonics because they have 'worked it out' for themselves, but the slower reader may require more systematic phonic teaching and exercises similar to the ones over the page. When children are sufficiently fluent, as a result of building up an adequate working sight vocabulary, then the teachings of phonics can be based on these sight words. Such words as 'bad', 'bag', 'back', 'bat', and 'bang' begin with the 'ba' sound. The children should be asked what sound is found at the beginning of each of these words. They should then be encouraged to find other words with the same beginning sound. In the same way, the children can discover the final sounds of consonants preceded by a vowel. Such words as 'can', 'fan', 'pan', 'ran', and 'man' end with the 'an' sound. When teaching the five vowel sounds the following sight words may be used:

> a as apple an and
>
> elephant egg end engine
>
> is in ink if into
>
> on off orange of
>
> up under us umbrella

Useful material at this stage:
The Programmed Reading Kit (Holmes McDougall)

Certain children will require pre-phonic activities and exercises. The teacher should see whether the child can recognise a word when she says its constituent sounds. If a child experiences difficulty with such words as 'bat', 'go', 'tap', 'sit' and 'pig', then the exercises on page 65 may be used.

Colour red the things beginning with B

Colour blue the things beginning with C

a Which word begins with a different sound from the others?

tap	cup	ten	tent
cap	dog	can	cup
fell	fox	fish	go
ran	rabbit	clock	rice
man	match	gate	mop
bat	balloon	bin	kite
six	seven	rat	sock

b Which word does not rhyme with the others?

bell	sell	shell	fall
fight	cow	light	night
goat	gun	boat	coat
chain	rain	hill	train
bill	fill	hill	fly
sail	shoe	mail	fail
engine	ball	fall	wall

c Letter sounds and phonic symbols.
Teach only a few letters at a time and revise frequently.
Start with letters which are easily distinguished from each other both by sound and appearance.
Leave the most similar until the last.
Use short periods of teaching.
(i) Flash cards containing letter or letter combinations. Emphasise differences between letter shapes.
(ii) When symbols can be identified by their sounds, ask the children to cut out pictures of objects from magazines whose names begin with the same sound.

d Blending sounds.
Use plastic letters or cards with single letters. Start with unvoiced consonants, e.g. f, s, n.
When the child has some ability in building words from letter sounds, he should have practice in his reading. It is wise to use reading material in which most of the words can be built up from letter sounds. This is provided in the *Royal Road Readers* (Chatto & Windus) Book 1, Part 1; Book 1, Part 2; 2A and 2B.

65

e   Phonic combinations.

These are dealt with systematically in the *Royal Road Readers,* but the readers need to be supplemented by other activities. Print a phonic combination on a card and then place it between consonants printed on larger cards, e.g. 'en' on a small card with b, t, d, m. The following words can be made: 'tent', 'bent', 'bend' and 'mend'.

Certain combinations may cause some difficulty. For example, 'ar', 'er', 'ir', 'ur' and 'or' are frequently confused with each other.

Useful phonic materials from Galt & Co. Ltd.:

Phonic Word Jigsaws
Phonic Self Teacher
Self-Checking Phonic Alphabet
Flannelgraph Phonic Reading Set

Teaching sounds with a pictorial alphabet

The use of a pictorial alphabet can assist children in their learning of initial sounds. The following pictorial alphabet shows how an attempt has been made to produce drawings of objects, animals, etc. in such a way that they represent the shapes of the initial letters of their names. When the pictorial alphabet is used, the association of an initial letter with a picture (as used in Stott's *Programmed Reading Kit*) is further assisted because the child may be able to remember the picture which is drawn in such a way that it represents the configuration of the initial letter. Various games and activities may be devised for the pictorial alphabet. The following pages show how sounds may be taught progressively.

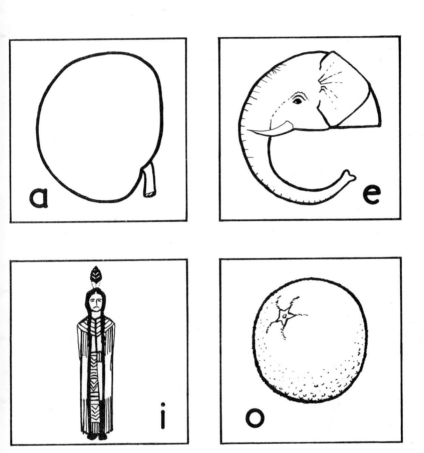

a

e

i

o

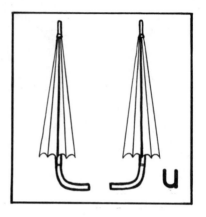

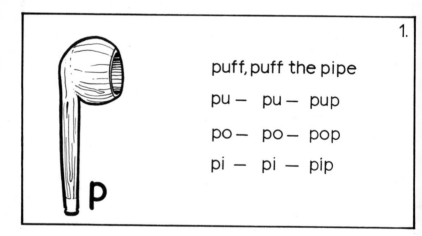

1.

puff, puff the pipe

pu — pu — pup

po — po — pop

pi — pi — pip

2.

ted— ted—teddy
to — to — tot
ti — ti — tit
ta — ta — tap
to — to — top
ti — ti — tip
tu — tu — tup

---

pa— pa— pat
po— po— pot
pe— pe— pet
pi — pi — pit

3.

ca — ca — cat
ca — ca — cap
co — co — cot
co — co — cop
cu — cu — cut
cu — cu — cup
ca— ca — can

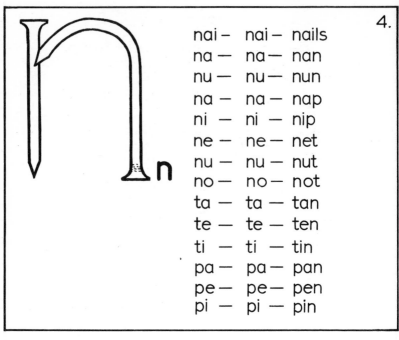

nai – nai – nails
na – na – nan
nu – nu – nun
na – na – nap
ni – ni – nip
ne – ne – net
nu – nu – nut
no – no – not
ta – ta – tan
te – te – ten
ti – ti – tin
pa – pa – pan
pe – pe – pen
pi – pi – pin

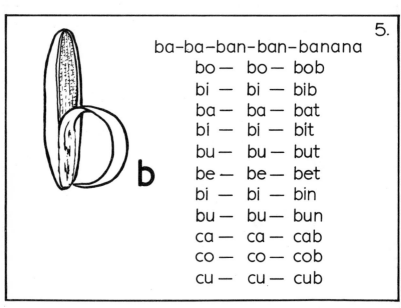

5.

ba–ba–ban–ban–banana
bo – bo – bob
bi – bi – bib
ba – ba – bat
bi – bi – bit
bu – bu – but
be – be – bet
bi – bi – bin
bu – bu – bun
ca – ca – cab
co – co – cob
cu – cu – cub

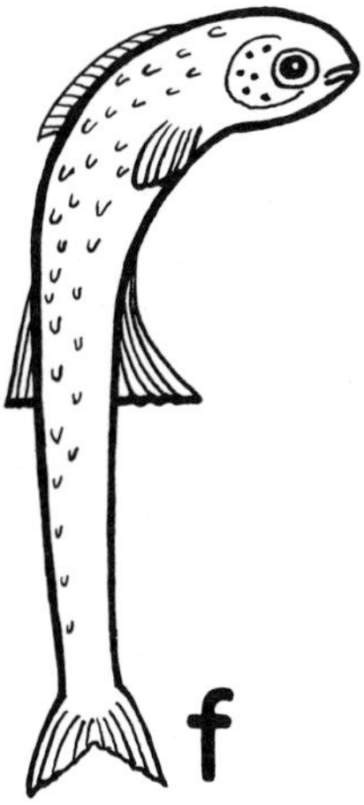

fi — fi — fish

fi — fi — fit

fa — fa — fat

fa — fa — fan

fi — fi — fin

fu — fu — fun

f

hor — hor — horse

ha — ha — hat

hi — hi — hit

ho — ho — hot

hi — hi — hip

ho — ho — hop

hu — hu — hut

hu — hu — hub

ho — ho — hob

h

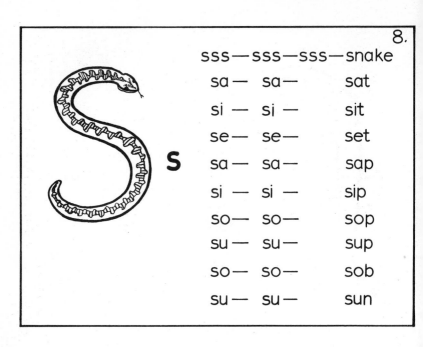

sss — sss — sss — snake

sa —	sa —	sat
si —	si —	sit
se —	se —	set
sa —	sa —	sap
si —	si —	sip
so —	so —	sop
su —	su —	sup
so —	so —	sob
su —	su —	sun

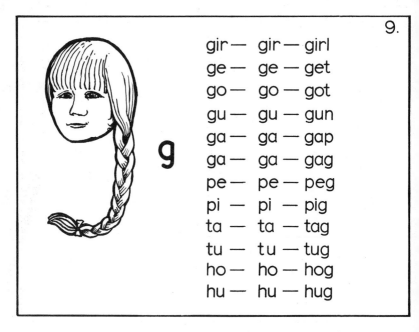

gir —	gir —	girl
ge —	ge —	get
go —	go —	got
gu —	gu —	gun
ga —	ga —	gap
ga —	ga —	gag
pe —	pe —	peg
pi —	pi —	pig
ta —	ta —	tag
tu —	tu —	tug
ho —	ho —	hog
hu —	hu —	hug

mit-tens mittens

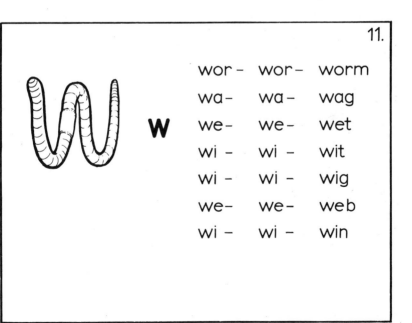

m

ma–	ma–	mat
me–	me–	met
ma–	ma–	man
me–	me–	men
ma–	ma–	map
mo–	mo–	mop
mu–	mu–	mug
am	am	am
ham	ham	ham
him	him	him
ram	ram	ram
Sam	Sam	Sam
sum	sum	sum

w

wor–	wor–	worm
wa–	wa–	wag
we–	we–	wet
wi –	wi –	wit
wi –	wi –	wig
we–	we–	web
wi –	wi –	win

The following illustrations may
be used for other sounds:

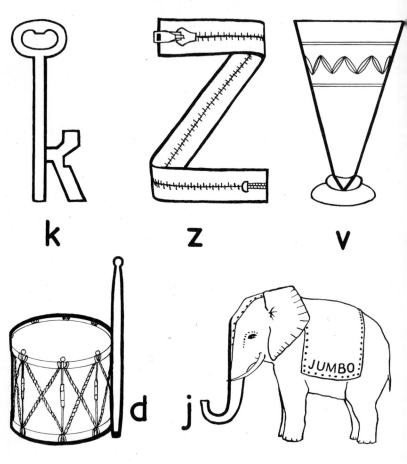

k   z   v

d j

Key words and word families

Key words are the most used words in English, applied to the vocabulary of the average person. In their book *Key Words to Literacy* McNally and Murray refer to research which has established that a relatively few English words form a very large proportion of those in daily use.

Many teachers have found that children read more easily and quickly if the first words they learn are the most used words of the language, and if these words are presented in attractive learning situations. Once these key words have been learned, many may be used as a basis for learning other words related to them, i.e. word families, and so expand the child's vocabulary by means of a phonic approach.

The following is a series of Word Family Worksheets designed to help the child to move from the 'known' sight word to other words containing the same basic sound combination. The worksheets may be used:

a On a one-to-one oral basis, i.e. the teacher allows the child to follow her finger as she points and reads out the words and then she asks him either to point at the correct word and say it aloud or to say the word without, at first, being asked to point at it;

b the teacher reads out the words and the child is asked to point at the correct word and print it in the space provided;

c the child completes the exercise without assistance from the teacher until the exercise is completed.

The following key words are used in the following exercises: see, and, looks, white, makes, small, came, right, went, been, other, well, back, down, soon, rain, sweet, coat, here, is, a, big, look, at, my, are, three, has, father, the, garden, see, in, fire, there, house, I, like, to, sleep, woman, can, these, this.

see
bee
tree
free
knee

Here is a big......

and
band
hand
sand
stand

Look at my......

looks
cooks
books
hooks
rooks

Here are three......

white
bite
site
mite
kite

Ben has a......

makes
cakes
takes
bakes
rakes

My father.......the
garden

small
call
tall
ball
fall

Here is a......

came
game
name
flame
same

right
light
fight
might
bright

See the.......in the fire

There is a.......in the house

went
tent
rent
bent
spent

been
seen
green
screen
keen

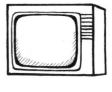

I like to sleep in a.......

This is a television........

other
brother
mother
another
smother

well
fell
bell
sell
shell

This woman is my........

This is a.......

back	down
sack	town
black	crown
pack	brown
rack	drown

This is a......   Here is a......

soon	rain
spoon	train
moon	chain
noon	pain
boon	drain

Look at this......   I can see the......

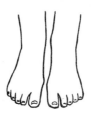

sweet	boat
feet	coat
meet	goat
sheet	float
sleet	stoat

Look at these two......   This animal is a......

Should there be an earlier start to reading?

There have been many heated arguments over the suggestion that reading may be taught before primary school age. Many educationists claim that a child will not normally be ready to read until he has reached a mental age of at least six years, and they suggest that it is extremely dangerous to attempt to accelerate the process because this will interfere with emotional and intellectual development. Many suggest that children are not ready for specific instruction in reading until a certain level of maturity has been reached. It has been said that if a child learns to read before going to school, he will become bored because he has to learn all over again, and, as a result, will put up a barrier against learning. There is a growing body of opinion, however, which believes that these dangers are overstated.

Is it true that children are incapable of learning to read before they have reached a mental age of six or six-and-a-half years?

Many who have studied reading problems have found that most children are not ready for specific instruction in reading before a certain state of maturity has been reached. The importance of the pre-reading period is continually stressed in professional literature. The first step to literacy is through speech, and it is essential for children to be able to build up a reservoir of ideas and vocabulary before a start in reading can be made. The importance of this statement has been stressed by many investigators, including Gates (1947), Monroe (1948), Schonell (1948), Malmquist (1958), Vernon (1958), Bernstein (1961), and Sampson (1962).

It has been suggested that if a child is faced with formal work in reading before he has had the experience to provide an adequate background of spoken language, then reading will lack significance for him. Schonell (1948) emphasises that reading develops from speech, and that it is fatal to force young children in their initial stages of learning to read, particularly if there have not been adequate activities to create a functional language background beforehand. Millard (1958) warns of forcing a child during the pre-reading period. 'Pressure tactics have varying effects if applied during a pre-readiness period and frustration or serious psychological damage may result.' McCullough et al. (1946) were concerned about pre-reading and reading readiness, and they say that if learning to read could be made more natural, more like the process by which a child learns to talk, fewer difficulties would appear later on. Robinson (1953) emphasises the importance of the pre-reading period in order to develop various phases of readiness prior to beginning reading instruction; and to explore visual, auditory, and emotional functions of beginning readers. Lovell (1963) states: 'An attempt to start to teach a child to read too early often frustrates him and helps to build up an emotional attitude against reading.'

It has been frequently suggested that many children of low mental age do not develop a work attitude until a mental age of about six and a half years, but there has been much disagreement over when a child should be ready to read, and the significance of mental age. P. E. Vernon (1960) says that a child should have 'crossed the initial hurdles in reading at about the mental age of eight'. Lovell (1963) says that most children in our society seem to be ready by about five-and-a-half to six years of age. Bruce (1964) studied the ability shown by children at different levels of mental development for the task of making a simple phonetic analysis of spoken words and concluded that a mental age of seven plus marks the point at which a real start is made on overcoming the difficulties encountered. Thackray (1965), in his research into the relationship between reading readiness and reading progress, found that in his sample of 182 children, a mental age of five-and-a-half was adequate for beginning to read and for making satisfactory progress in the early stages of reading. There are, however, many critics of those who specify a certain age at which a child should begin to read. Watts (1948) insists that the age at which a child wants to read depends not only on mental age, but the cultural background of the home, and the influence and enthusiasm of the teacher. Olson (Harris, 1957) states: 'Since children grow at widely varying rates, it is impossible to say that they will be ready for a particular experience at a specific age.'

Millard (1958) challenges the view held by most teachers regarding the meaning and significance of mental age. He says that mental age has always been looked upon as a criterion of performance. He says that if a child has a mental age of six-and-a-half he is said to be ready to begin reading. If he has a mental age of ten he is expected to do the school work normally expected of a child of ten. He goes on to say that in making such judgments, it is immaterial whether the first child mentioned has a chronological age of five, six or seven years. 'Although two children may have a mental age of six-and-a-half when they are six-and-a-half chronologically, one child may have a greater maturity at the time. Such difference in children serves to challenge the validity of the mental age readiness concept and suggests the possibility of maturity as a more effective criterion.'

Gesell (1954) and Gesell (Carmichael, 1954) seemed very definitely to be of the opinion that maturation is of great importance. He said that maturation seems to limit, to a great extent, an individual's rate of learning and to determine his ultimate levels of achievement. Olson (Harris, 1957) states: 'The maturation process describes the potential capacities of the individual, but experience determines the expression in development.'

Millard says that there appear to be definite degrees of maturity necessary for various kinds of learning and suggests that if a teacher tries to force learning in advance of essential general maturity she may be setting up an inhibitory situation which may immediately affect the child's personality in such a way as to cause him to rebel against learning when 'the time for its natural beginning arrives.'

Downing (1963), however, discussing the findings of research into i.t.a., suggests that further research may indicate that the mental age required for reading readiness may prove to be much closer to that needed for 'learning to listen and to speak with understanding than many educators have thought in the past'.

More and more educators are emphasising the importance of maturation as a factor affecting reading readiness. The general opinion has been that before learning can proceed with maximum efficiency the learner must have reached a necessary degree of maturity. The degrees of maturity represent periods of readiness for learning when a minimum of training and practice will produce the greatest returns in achievement. Chronological and mental ages are not the sole accurate indicators of readiness; children develop at different rates. A favourable environment offering opportunities for spontaneous learning will encourage the onset of reading readiness; deprivation will delay it. With all this in mind, we, as teachers of reading, must accept that the reading process is an individual and personal matter, and appreciate that a child will express his personality in the manner in which he reads, and in the point in his development when he starts to read.

There is now a growing body of evidence to prove that children learn to read before the chronological or mental age of six.

The First International Reading Symposium has provided ample evidence.

R. Lynn has shown that the development of the perceptual abilities needed for reading depends on learning and not on maturation. The physiological development of a child is not necessarily immature before the age of six. He suggests that a mental age of two-and-a-half to three-and-a-half years is sufficient for the perception and learning of words without any detrimental effects, providing that the environment provides sufficiently stimulating experiences.

Professor Durkin carried out an experiment at the University of Illinois which involved a carefully controlled comparison of thirty children who had learned to read before six years with those who had learned later. By the end of the third year of schooling, the early readers were still one year ahead on average. Durkin found that all the parents of the early readers had noticed that their children had taken an interest in reading before the age of four. All these parents had assisted their children in identifying letters, numbers, words and sounds. But above all, they had spent time answering their children's many questions and discussing the meanings of words. The parents of the late readers generally accepted that reading should be taught by a teacher in the school. These parents were also too busy to respond to the possibility that their children were ready to learn to read.

Sutton (1966) suggests that children can benefit from an early start in reading, and Mason and Prater (1966) conclude that early training in reading is both possible and profitable, especially the training in word recognition. *But* it must be emphasised that not all children can start reading at an earlier age. Doman (1963) probably goes to the extreme when he suggests that all should learn to read when they are babies. Many children with low intelligence and linguistic deprivation will not read before the age of six or even later. What is most important is that individual differences in the capacities and experiences of children are catered for. Those children who read early do so usually because of sufficient innate capacities, the abilities acquired as a result of stimulating experiences in their pre-school environments and suitable school conditions.

If children can obtain satisfaction when their curiosity is at its strongest then this should benefit their progress in later years. If a child learns to read early he will gain an advantage not only in reading ability, but in the whole world that reading opens up. If a child can be taught to read early this is especially important for the slow learning child. Frequently, but not always, a quick learning child with a high IQ who had not learned to read early might catch up on those who had.

A five-year study financed by the US Office of Education involved over 4,000 children in Denver, Colorado. It investigated beginning reading instruction in the kindergarten and how it affected pupils' subsequent reading performance. A comparison was made between the effectiveness of beginning reading teaching in the kindergarten with beginning reading in the first grade. Several groups of activities were used with the kindergarten children.

These were:

a using spoken context
b listening for letter sounds
c distinguishing letter forms
d using spoken context and sound clues together
e using spoken context and the first letter in a printed word

It was concluded that beginning reading skills can be taught effectively to large numbers of kindergarten children. The permanence of gain depended upon subsequent teaching. The earlier reading influenced achievement in other areas where success depended upon reading proficiency.

Methods used in teaching pre-school children to read

It has been claimed that all children in Montessori schools learn to read and write before the normal school age. It is interesting to note a few of the approaches used in these schools. The teachers start the 'I Spy' game as early as possible. 'This is the letter B. Can you see anything beginning with the letter B? I spy a box. B is for box.' Gradually the children appreciate the sound of the letter. The children are given sandpaper letters which they use to trace over with their fingers so that they can learn the shapes. This helps them when they begin writing. Another approach is to give the child pictures and coloured, sandpaper-covered letters. The child looks at two or three pictures and he may select a picture of a cat. The child sounds the word cat and then, still repeating the initial 'c' sound, he finds the sandpaper-covered 'c'. He puts the letter 'c' near the picture. Then he finds the 'a', then the 't', sounding out each letter as he finds it. The child then continues to build up the words for the other pictures, and deals with 'hat' and 'man'. If a child encounters a letter and he cannot remember the sound then he asks for help. If he cannot remember the initial sound in 'pan', the parent or teacher finds a sandpaper-covered letter 'p' and guides the child's finger-tips over the shape of 'p', while she repeats the sound of the letter. So the child learns the sound through his fingers, eyes and ears. Certain teachers have suggested that parents could assist their children along the 'reading road' by teaching the alphabet using large wooden or plastic letters and making up games with them. When the alphabet is mastered, it is suggested that children should be taught to read simple words rather than sentences. These simple words should be concrete nouns—names of objects which the child can see, touch and feel. Labels can be pasted on these objects.

A well-tried 'sight-word' method used in the United States is the Doman-Delcato method. A child is shown a large card with two-inch high red letters printed on it. He is casually told what the word is. This is done on a few occasions throughout the day. Later he is given the card and asked what the word says. If he is correct, he is praised and fun is made of the achievement. The parent exhibits a burst of enthusiasm. If he cannot remember he is told the word once again. There is no criticism on the part of the parent. The words may include 'Mummy', 'Daddy' and the child's name. The parents use cards of smaller size when the child has learnt about thirty words. As the child progresses, he eventually reads words of beginner-reader size.

Beck (1968) describes how, in 1964, the *Chicago Tribune* decided to develop a comic strip feature to help teach pre-school children to read at home. Mrs Dorothy Watson, a nursery school teacher, developed an approach based on a phonic plan. The approach included many games and activities:

The parent shows the child a large letter 'h' in the comic strip and she emphasises that the letter looks like a chair. The next frame on the comic strip shows a boy running. The mother reads, 'Harry ran home so fast, he was out of breath.' Then, looking at the next frame, she says, 'He fell in the chair, and all he could say was h–h–h–h–h.' Then the mother encourages the child to run across the room, pretend to be out of breath and fall into an h-shaped chair making the out-of-breath 'h' sound.

Finally, the mother asks the child to listen for the 'h' sound as she says such words as house, hammer, horse, hat and hop. She then asks the child to think of words the child may know beginning with the out-of-breath sound—'h', and she writes them down. It is suggested at this stage that there is no need to teach the names of the letters first, except for the vowels, which frequently have the sound of their names.

The second comic strip teaches 'm', linking the sound with such names as milk, mouse, money, monkey and moon, and the shape of a pair of child's mittens. The next stage is to introduce 'p'. This is related to the noise of Papa making a puffing sound with his pipe. The mother writes down several words beginning with the 'p' sound and she asks the child to draw a ring around each 'p' as she sounds out the words. It is emphasised that the games should only be played for a few minutes at a time and the child must *want* to play. It is suggested that each period should be one minute for each year of the child's age, but a few periods a day can be used. The child is encouraged to look for letter sounds elsewhere, e.g. labels, newspapers, cereal packets, etc.

The next stage is to teach the 's' sound and this is associated with snake. This is followed by the 'w' sound. The child is encouraged to hold his hand in front of his mouth and say such 'windy sounds' as watch, win, wig and witch.

The letter 't' is learned in association with the t–t–t–t–t–t tick of the clock, and 'r' is associated with the r–r–r–r–r–r of a noisy dog.

It is suggested that when the child has learned the sounds and shapes of these six consonants then he is ready for his first vowel sound. The 'a' as in apple is taught first. A very important stage is reached when the child is able to blend consonants and vowels and so make the first word. A comic strip shows a child rolling 'h' and 'a', and 't' into a snowball. When the child reaches the eighth comic strip, he is able to read a very simple comic using only the sounds he has learned and is able to blend together. For the remainder of the thirteen-week series, the child receives a comic every day to read to himself. These also contain new sounds. The child reads comics and plays simple games based on the letter shapes or sounds of 'j', 'l', 'z', 'b' and 'd'. These are followed by 'e' as in egg, 'ck'—the 'k' sound as in duck and 'g' (both hard and soft sounds). It is suggested that the mother should play simple games using the basic sounds. A bingo card can be used, with letters instead of numbers and small sweets or counters as markers. The mother says the sounds and the child calls out when he has covered a row.

The child learns a few digraphs when he has learned the consonants and short vowel sounds—sh, ch and th. This is eventually followed by common letter combinations such as 'all', 'ook', 'ight', 'ank' and 'ink'. This helps the child learn irregular vowel sounds and consonant combinations. These common letter combinations are then blended with known initial consonant sounds.

The next stage is to teach vowel names. The following rules are taught:

Two vowels coming together in a word or having only one letter in between in a short word—then the first one usually says its own name and the second one remains silent. Eventually, the child applies the rule to 'kit'—'kite', 'man'—'mane', 'mat'—'mate', 'bit'—'bite' and 'not'—'note'. Obviously, the child will encounter many words which are phonically irregular. It is suggested that these should be taught as sight words.

Many critics of the 'early to read approach' say that a three- or four- or five-year-old will suffer intellectually, emotionally and physically if allowed to read. Some say that these children will develop 'eye strain'. But it is not surprising how very young children discover very small objects such as buttons, pins and small beads on chairs and on the floor? Early reading does not appear to have a detrimental effect on a child's eyesight if large and clear letters are used. Another argument is that very young children are unable to discriminate between sounds. But is there not a tremendous amount of auditory discrimination involved in language learning?

In conclusion, I would suggest that many children, but not all, can and should learn to read earlier if (i) the initial reading activities are enjoyed by the child and they satisfy his needs; (ii) it is remembered that the individual differences between children will determine these initial reading activities, and (iii) there are favourable environmental conditions.

Chapter 4

The teaching of spelling

There is no doubt that English spelling creates many difficulties for children and adults but, today, we are not so concerned over these difficulties. Most educated people learn to spell the majority of English words in everyday use but we are now much more aware that intelligent adults are liable to make spelling errors, even in fairly simple and well-known words. But this does not mean that certain basic skills should be ignored.

Informal approaches to teaching in primary schools have resulted in a reaction against formal spelling lessons. Certain teachers and advisers suggest that children make progress in spelling quite incidentally through reading, writing and many other activities. Probably this attitude is a reaction against the formal 'spelling period'—usually every Friday morning—when children were tested on lists of words learned by heart. Many of these words were unrelated to the words the children actually used or to the words they required for reading, writing and other activities.

Many teachers believe that the teaching of spelling occurs incidentally when children are encouraged to write about their interests or report on topics or themes studied during the schoolday, resulting in an enlargement of vocabulary. Many are convinced that spelling is a means to an end and that it should be a servant of creative writing. Frequently, there is little evidence of actual instruction but occasionally teachers' comments highlight their dilemma in relation to the teaching of spelling. This dilemma arises because, in the past, spelling together with reading and writing has been associated with 'formal teaching'. Unfortunately, 'formal teaching' mistakenly, in my opinion, too often implies certain methods such as stereotyped instruction, drill and rote learning, and this is anathema to teachers trained and brought up in a contemporary child-centred school climate. These teachers do not wish to discourage their pupils' free writing by using too much red ink on spelling errors. There is also a fear that if one forces some children to make their written work more readable by too much concentration on correct spelling, they may exhibit a reluctance to put pencil or pen to paper. There is no doubt that writing can become a very painful experience if the child is committed to a mental effort for almost every word that he writes.

A child involved in an eleven-plus system and intensive streaming was severely handicapped if he could not spell correctly. Today, with the gradual disappearance of the eleven-plus, spelling has lost some of its intimidating qualities. But many teachers believe that spelling still has some importance, although some are not sure what. These teachers console themselves with the belief that spelling can be 'picked up' quite incidentally while the children are engrossed in 'very important activities' such as creative writing. But is spelling 'picked up' so easily, and, if so, by how many children? Practice is of utmost importance when a child is learning a skill like reading or spelling. Talk of insight and discovery is valid in relation to the learning of concepts in mathematics and science but talk of insight has very little point when a child is confronted with the anomalies and inconsistencies of English spelling. Maybe it is unrealistic to expect perfection in spelling from all children, particularly slow learners, but surely it is reasonable to expect teachers to try to eradicate errors in the spelling of words of common usage and so make their written work more intelligible.

If spelling is poor and careless, communication suffers because the reader is constantly held up through having to puzzle out what a word is. There is no doubt that the degree of accuracy necessary in spelling is closely connected with ease of communication. Correct spelling is an exercise in self-discipline, because it is a skill requiring accuracy, and accuracy is generally one of the main virtues that educated people should have. It involves acquiring a habit of care and attention which manifests itself in handwriting and the construction of sentences.

Certain teachers are less likely to be critical of the spelling, punctuation and sentence construction in a child's writing if the content is 'creative', exciting and vivid. But surely we are only free to write with confidence when our spelling is automatic and predictable. Surely the competent and confident speller is in a better position to explore new ways of expressing himself. Such a child will experiment with new words used, first of all, in conversation and then in writing. The poor speller may avoid using these new and exciting words. There is a danger that he will use less precise words to convey his thoughts. Children and adults do not necessarily exhibit freedom to write creatively by ignoring spelling. The informal approach has its virtues but many children, especially slow learners, have difficulties in spelling and incidental learning is inadequate for these children. A systematic approach has to be adopted.

So spelling is an essential skill if children are to be able to write freely and adventurously without hesitation. Can spelling be caught, or must it be taught? If it can be caught, why is it that such a large number of children from primary schools find spelling such a difficult exercise and are frequently unable to spell very simple words? If spelling should be taught, what methods can be used? But, first of all, what are the factors influencing spelling ability?

Factors associated with spelling ability

Schonell (1959) says that spelling is a complex sensory motor process 'the efficiency of which is based on repeated motor reaction to sensory stimuli. Perceptual impression, auditory and visual, must fuse with motor responses, articulatory and graphic, to ensure mastery over words'.

Normally a child with unimpaired sense equipment learns a new word by adopting an analytic-synthetic procedure. Schonell suggests that the word is first perceived as a whole and then the child notes the characteristic or its configuration. Then it is divided up into its syllables. The syllables are linked with their correct sounds by vocalisation so that auditory-articulatory association is formed. Then the parts are related to the whole.

Many children are able to 'break down' and 'build up' almost unconsciously but some have to make it a more conscious activity. Other children may have to pay particular attention to phonic families, irregular sound values and various peculiarities of visual form. Writing activities cement the visual, auditory and articulatory elements in words.

What causes disability in spelling? What makes a person a good speller? There is no single answer to these questions. Some children cannot spell because of physiological defects; some cannot spell because they lack motivation; some are good

89

spellers because they have had favourable environments. Organic defects can prevent muscular co-ordination in the case of children with neurological impairment, as in cerebral palsied children. There are many children who are unable to copy correctly due to delays in the development of perceptual skills. A detailed study of causal factors can be found in *Backwardness in the Basic Subjects* (Schonell, 1959).

The main causes of poor spelling relate to the senses. Schonell summarises the general conditions connected with disability in spelling as follows:

a   Weakness in visual perception of words for both discrimination and span.

b   Weakness in auditory analysis and synthesis of verbal material. There may be a combination of (a) and (b) in some cases.

c   Weakness in general intelligence, together with some perceptual deficiency.

d   Sensory defects, particularly visual defects.

e   Faulty pronunciation.

f   Temperamental attitudes, particularly variation in attitudes towards correctness of detail.

g   Emotional inhibitions.

h   Environmental conditions, such as absence from school, frequent change of school, bad teaching methods.

Two factors rank very high on this list, i.e. (a) and (b). The child's ears and eyes may be efficient organically, but he still may not be able to hear or see efficiently.

It appears that efficient imagery plays a very important part in correct spelling and that certain brain rhythms and certain forms of imagery go together. We certainly rely on visual imagery in spelling. (Peters, in her book *Spelling—Caught or Taught* [1967], gives an excellent survey of the problems and approaches to spelling.)

Methods of teaching spelling

There are several methods of teaching spelling. Some teachers teach spelling incidentally and hope for an association between reading and spelling ability. There is no doubt that many children learn to spell incidentally through various experiences, but more attention must be paid to the systematic teaching of spelling—this is particularly important if one wishes to show children how they can teach themselves. Any approach adopted by a teacher should take into consideration the strengths and weaknesses of children's sensory channels and visual, auditory, articulatory and kinaesthetic methods should all be used.

The early teaching of spelling should include an approach which allows children to see the word, read it correctly and pay particular attention to its specific characteristic. It is important that the child enunciates the word clearly and the teacher should set an example. The children may be encouraged to write the word in a sand tray, or with their fingers on the desk or in the air. Naturally, it is extremely important that children appreciate the meaning and use of the word. A valuable exercise is to write the word on the blackboard and allow the child to study it for a certain period of time—writing it in the air, in sand, etc. Then the word should be covered up so that immediate recall is required. It is very important to encourage the child to look at a word and try to retain a visual image of it. Such an exercise is an important part of diagnosis. Some children may require additional exercises to assist them and the teacher may have to provide word-cards containing words made of glue with sand sprinkled on them. The teacher may have to provide sandpaper letters for some children.

The idea of self-image is posed by Peters as having a significant part to play in producing good spelling ability. It is probably when children are motivated to pay attention to the structures of words, to retain the perception, to follow practices of self-testing, to produce with pride a well-presented piece of work, that they are going to discipline themselves to become good spellers. Motivation at such a rigorous level does not depend on externally imposed incentives of immediate rewards, not on the desire to conform, not even to communicate courteously, but on the self-image the individual has of himself as a good speller.

If early perceptual training in learning to read such as looking at a picture, repeating the word printed underneath or repeating a sentence underneath, encourages the perceptual technique, it seems logical to assume that spelling skill can also be taught by systematic methods because spelling depends so much on perceptual habits. There is a danger that haphazard methods that consist mainly of incidental learning will be detrimental. Incidental learning resulting from creativeness, discovery and experimental methods should be reinforced by using a specific method of learning to spell. Unfortunately, the systematic teaching of spelling is becoming increasingly rare but it must be remembered that the creative qualities of free writing depend on giving more attention to spelling.

From the infant school onwards the children's attention should be drawn to the patterns of letters in words, the visual structure of words—and this can be done through the use of various games. One can begin with words that have the same pattern and sound alike, then words that have the same internal pattern but do not sound alike. This can be done through the use of pictures with the words to strengthen the imagery involved in recall. Children should be provided with their own individual spelling books which they compile and build up with words they have learned or wish to learn. Simple dictionaries are also essential and children should be taught how to use them. It is important that these dictionaries contain the correct vocabulary. Many teachers construct wall-dictionaries and attach strips of card to a curtain rail. Words may be collected from the children's writing. These words can be classified and grouped according to difficulty. Such word lists can be given to groups of children to learn. Individual children can learn from the lists they have compiled in their word books. If we adopt this approach we will ensure that the words being learned will be within the particular vocabulary of particular children. After all, there is little point in learning words that may never be used in the future.

The teacher should read the words to certain groups of children so that they fully understand their pronunciations. Comprehension is essential and these words should be put in sentences. It is at this time that the teacher will comment on particular characteristics and difficulties and suggest possible ways of remembering certain parts of words.

Spelling rules may be useful but it must be remembered that these do not necessarily have wide application.

1　'i' is before 'e' except after 'c'.
　　'i' before 'e' except after 'c' when the sound of the letters is 'ee'.

2　If a word ends in 'y' and is preceded by a consonant it changes the 'y' into 'i' before adding an ending, unless the ending begins with 'i', e.g. busy, business.

3　If a word ends in a consonant and it has a single vowel before it, double the consonant before adding an ending, if the ending begins with a vowel, e.g. shop, shopping.

4　If a word ends in 'e' it usually drops the 'e' when an

ending is added if the ending begins with a vowel, e.g. shine, shining.

5   If words end in a consonant followed by 'e', the preceding vowel is pronounced with the *name* of the letter, e.g. spade.

6   If a vowel comes before a double consonant it is pronounced with the *sound* of the letter. A vowel coming before a single consonant is usually pronounced with the *name* of the letter, e.g. latter, later.

7   A word ending in 'y' with a consonant before it, changes the 'y' to 'i' to make the plural and adds 'es', e.g. baby, babies.

8   A word ending in 'f' sometimes changes the 'f' into 'v' and adds 'es' to form the plural, e.g. leaf, leaves.

A logical time to begin the systematic teaching of spelling is with the teaching of phonics. After all, writing and spelling words correctly are additional aids to phonics. The ability to spell varies from child to child, therefore the approach should take into account individual differences. Class teaching is not efficient when one has to deal with large classes even if these classes are streamed. These individual differences in ability make it necessary to use various approaches to the perceiving of words. Slow children will require a teaching method based on a visual, auditory, kinaesthetic and tactile approach. Those slower children who suffer from poor visual perception should receive additional exercises in copying and remembering phonically irregular words.

Tansley (1967) suggests an assignment technique for the teaching of spelling to slow learners but the technique can be useful for all children. The general principles of this technique are as follows:

1   A set of graded assignments—each of not more than fifteen words. (The 110 assignments are used from *Sound Sense*—Teacher's Book). Assignments are related to a phonic programme but they include phonically irregular words in common usage.

2   Children are grouped in pairs as a result of a standardised spelling test.

3   Each pair receives an assignment. This matches their spelling level or is just below it.

4   Assignments are copied in the child's handwriting. The

teacher ensures that the copy is correct and that the child can read and pronounce each word accurately.

5 Children study the assignment words as follows:

a The children look at a word, working independently; they say the word and try to memorise its visual form. They try to write it without looking at the word. They check their response against the correct spelling. The procedure is repeated until the word is known. Each word is studied in this way.

b The children test each other when all the words have been studied. A word is given, then the child writes and says the words. Spelling is checked by the partner.

c When the children can spell every word, the teacher tests them.

d The teacher asks each child to write sentences which illustrate the meaning of the words. Oral sentences may also be accepted in certain cases.

e The above method is repeated on the next assignment.

Assessment of spelling ability

There are many difficulties involved in the diagnosis of specific weaknesses in spelling and Peters emphasises the dangers of making assumptions based on superficial evidence. The following tests are frequently used:

1 Burt's Graded Spelling Vocabulary Test in *Mental and Scholastic Tests* (Staples Press, 1921).

2 Schonell's Spelling Tests S1, S2 in *Diagnostic and Attainment Testing* (Oliver & Boyd, 1950).

3 Lambert's *Seven Plus Assessment* (ULP, 1951). 7–8 years.

4 Daniels and Diack's Standard Spelling Test, in *Standard Reading Tests* (Chatto & Windus, 1958).

Standardised tests of spelling ability can be used on a class basis and a spelling age calculated, but one must make certain reservations regarding the validity of the results because considerable time may have elapsed since these tests were standardised (see Burt's). So many tests may be questioned on the grounds of age, reliability and standardisation. It has been suggested that standardised tests are useful because (a) the results can help in the grouping of children; (b) a comparison can be made between a child's mental age and his reading age; (c) diagnostic information can be obtained from a study of the types of errors being made and (d) a child's spelling age will help the teacher decide on the words to be taught. One should seriously examine certain claims for such tests.

Some analysis of the spelling errors of children should be carried out. These errors may be classified as follows:

1 Omissions, e.g. softy for softly.
2 Transpositions, e.g. parm for pram.
3 Putting in extra letters, e.g. indiain for indian.
4 Doubling, e.g. spitefull for spiteful.
5 Using incorrect letters.
6 Visual confusion, e.g. gian for gain.
7 Substitutions, e.g. thay for they.
8 Phonetic spelling, e.g. skool for school.
9 Errors due to poor speech, e.g. bruvver for brother.

Chapter 5

Reading schemes

The early books of certain reading schemes are frequently dull, boring and over-repetitive. Reading schemes cannot make use of children's various interests in the same way as a teacher can when she is making books with the children. Various graded reading schemes are useful for the slow child but, with the better reader, it is more important to use books dealing with various topics and themes. The teacher must ensure that children are using books which are not too difficult otherwise they may become so discouraged that they put up a reading barrier. Frequently, one may encounter a child who has been 'labouring' away at the same book week after week.

During the initial stages of learning to read, children should be given the opportunity to learn as many as possible of the new words they will meet in a new book before they actually begin reading it. This is an attempt at ensuring that their progress through the new book will be fairly quick and the initial success will engender further success. Books should be so arranged in the classroom that the teacher, and particularly the children, will appreciate their appropriate reading levels. A colour coding system may be adopted so that children are easily guided to the appropriate books. Children may be provided with book-markers that carry a colour code that matches the colour code used for the books.

A graded reading scheme is intended to provide reading material that will provide graded steps through the basic steps of reading until the child reaches a stage when he can 'blossom forth' and tackle a wider range of reading materials. The intention behind a well-planned, graded reading scheme is to provide graded books of gradually increasing difficulty with smaller, parallel supplementary books at approximately the same level of difficulty planned to widen a child's reading experience and to consolidate reading. One can rarely get sufficient practice at each level reached by using one reading scheme. There should be a wide range of books and supplementary materials. A teacher may decide that a child needs to read more books at a certain level of reading ability before moving on to the next step in a graded series. A graded book guide is useful in helping the teacher to find appropriate reading material for children at different levels of reading attainment. Here is a selection of guides:

Help in Reading (National Book League)

Words of Persuasion (Cambridge University Press)

Children's Reading (Univ. of Leeds Inst. of Ed. Paper no. 8)

It has been found that if a child is kept on one reading scheme without the opportunity to sample other reading experiences, then this is detrimental to the child's development of independence in reading and his overall reading growth. It is common, today, to provide children with a wide variety of reading material containing books from various reading schemes and books for general reading.

A reading scheme containing a graded series helps the teacher organise a class with a wide range of reading attainment. As a child moves through the reading scheme, he provides the teacher with evidence of his progress. Furthermore, a graded series provides a control over the grading of vocabulary and content.

A reading scheme may be regarded as complementary to the teaching of various reading skills. Many publishers of reading schemes provide supplementary material. This material is a means of helping the child become accustomed to the characters and words that he will eventually meet in his first reading books.

A good reading scheme should consist of good and genuine stories. Furthermore, the incidents and language in the early books should be within the child's experience so that present day interests are catered for and the words used are within the natural conversation of children. The early books should contain large and clear print. The letter shapes should be consistent. The early books should contain a fairly short word list. There should be an adequate number of new words to a page and these new words should be carefully controlled with adequate repetition to help the children memorise them.

The first books of the reading scheme should not be too long and they should offer relatively quick success which should engender further success. The steps between one book and the next should be gradual. The illustrations should be good and not distorted, and should be helpful to the reading of the text. These illustrations should be appropriate to the age of the child and relevant to the age in which we are living. The covers of the books should be brightly covered, durable and well-bound. The print should be good, large and clear, especially for the first books, with not too many words on one page. There should be consistency in letter shapes. It should also be noted whether the books are girl-biased or boy-biased. Girls will usually accept boys' books but boys will only rarely accept girls' books.

Useful information on reading schemes may be obtained from the following sources:

1 Centre for the Teaching of Reading, 29 Eastern Avenue, Reading.

2 *Reading Schemes—their Emphases and their Interchangeability*. Cambridge Institute of Education, Shaftesbury Avenue, Cambridge.

3 *Reading Schemes for Slow Learners*. Child Guidance Service, 12 Grange Road, West Bromwich.

A selection of reading schemes

1 *Adventures in Reading* by G. Keir (Oxford University Press)
Reading age: 5–9 years   Interest age: 7–12 years
Intended for slow readers.
Six readers with a supplementary reader for each.
Six workbooks.
Three crossword puzzle books.
Additional material for older pupils.
Teacher's guide.
Approach: 'look and say'.

2 *The Griffin Readers* by S. K. McCullagh (E. J. Arnold)
Reading age: 5–8 years   Interest age: 6–12 years
Twelve graded readers with supplementary readers.
Workbooks.
Teacher's guide.
Approach: 'whole word'.

3 *The Ladybird Key Words Reading Scheme* by W. Murray (Wills & Hepworth)
Reading age: 5–9 years   Interest age: 5–9 years

Thirty-six readers in three parallel sets.
Workbooks.
Large and small flash cards, picture-word and picture-sentence matching cards, outline picture pads and picture dictionaries.
Teacher's guide.
Approach: Mixed. Emphasis on sentence method at the beginning followed by phonics later.

4 *Janet and John Reading Scheme* by M. O'Donnell and R. Munro (James Nisbet)
Reading age: 5–8 years   Interest age: 5–11 years
Six readers (two series—phonic or 'whole word').
Eight extension readers.
Supplementary readers.
Story books.
Four workbooks.
Comprehension cards, picture dictionary, pictures, flash cards, sentence book, word-matching, picture-word and picture-sentence matching cards, outline picture pads, coloured cut-out pictures, lotto sets, jigsaw, pictorial rubber stamp, cellograph and stand-up figures.
Teacher's guide.
Approach: Mixed. (One phonic series and one 'whole word' series).

5 *The Happy Venture Reading Scheme* by F. J. Schonell, I. Sergeant and P. Flowerdew (Oliver & Boyd)
Reading age: 5–8 years   Interest age: 5–10 years
Five readers.
Five playbooks.
Library books.
Five workbooks.
Flash cards, wall pictures, filmstrips, word and picture stamps, colouring book, jigsaws, rubber stamps, stand-up figures, cellograph and lotto cards.
Teacher's guide.
Approach: Mixed but with 'look and say' bias.

6 *The McKee Reading Scheme* by P. McKee, M. L. Harrison, A. McCowen and E. Lehr (Thomas Nelson)
Reading age: 5–8 years   Interest age: 8–11 years

Five readers.
McKee Platform Readers (supplementary material).
Four sets with six titles in each.
Three workbooks for Books 3, 4 and 5.
Flash cards, wall pictures, outline pictures for colouring.
Teacher's guide for each level.
Approach: Mixed but with early introduction of phonics.

7 *Gay Way Series* by E. R. Boyce (Macmillan)
Reading age: 5–8 years   Interest age: 5–10 years
Six graded readers.
Three intermediate books.
Six sets of supplementary readers (four titles in each).
Four workbooks.
Nursery rhyme pictures and picture books, picture dictionary and song book.
Approach: Mixed but with a phonic bias.

8 *Racing to Read/Sound Sense*
Racing to Read by A. E. Tansley and R. H. Nicholls
Sound Sense by A. E. Tansley (E. J. Arnold)
Reading age: 5–9 years   Interest age: 5–11 years
Suitable for slow readers.
Sixteen *Racing to Read* story readers.
Eight *Sound Sense* books with an emphasis on phonic exercises.
Teacher's guide.
Approach: Mixed when both are used.

9 *The Royal Road Readers* by J. C. Daniels and H. Diack (Chatto and Windus)
Reading age: 5–9 years   Interest age: 7–15 years
Twelve readers (nine stages).
Supplementary books for each stage.
Other supplementary materials from Philip & Tacey.
Teacher's guide.
Approach: Phonic 'whole word'. The use of these words in such a way as to ensure that the child appreciates function of letters.

10 *Words in Colour* by C. Gattegno (Cuisenaire Co. Ltd.)
Reading age: 5–7 years   Interest age: 5 + years

Three readers.
Wall charts.
Book of stories, word building book, work sheets.
Teacher's guide.
Approach: Phonic using colour.

11 *Reading by Rainbow* by E. and W. Bleasdale (Moor Platt Press)
Intended to supplement other reading schemes.
Four readers.
Two supplementary books for second and third stages.
Eight worksheets.
Reference cards—letter-sound drawings.
Teacher's guide.
Approach: Phonic using four colours.

12 *Step up and Read* by W. R. Jones (ULP)
Reading age: 6–9 years   Interest age: 8–14 years
Intended as a remedial scheme.
Phonic cards—programmed graded steps.
Stories starting with a strictly phonic vocabulary and then eventually involving an unrestricted vocabulary.
Exercises for each phonic stage, picture-word matching, exercises with phrases and sentences.
Teacher's guide.
Approach: Phonic.

13 *Sounds and Words* by V. Southgate and J. Havenhand (ULP)
Reading age: 5–9 years   Interest age: 8–13 years
Six graded readers.
Eight supplementary readers (four stories in each).
Teacher's guide.
Approach: Phonic.

14 *The Downing Readers* by J. Downing (Initial Teaching Publishing Co. Ltd.)
Ten introductory readers.
Two readers.
Four readers—vocabulary extension series.
Large flash cards, auditory discrimination cards, wall picture book and large sentence book, word matching

cards, picture-sentence matching cards, word building cards, flannelgraph cut-outs and character matching cards.

Teacher's guide.

Approach: Using i.t.a. as a medium—'look and say' at the beginning but has a phonic bias.

Chapter 6

Classroom organisation

When one considers that one must attempt to meet the needs of individuals and fully appreciate that they develop at different rates, and that some learn to read more easily in one particular way and others more easily by another, then one has to consider the problem involved in organising the reading activities.

Many teachers complain of large classes and continually ask the question—'How can I cater for the slow readers in a class of thirty-eight?' Sympathy and understanding are extended to these teachers but, in spite of large classes, many teachers have carried out quite amazing work with very limited equipment.

In the first junior class there may be older and more mature children who are quite fluent in reading but there may be others who have only progressed a little through the reading scheme used in their infant school. The older and more mature children may have a fairly adequate knowledge of phonics but the slower children may not have reached the 'phonic stage' adopted in their particular infant school. There may also be a few children who have not made a real start in reading.

Before one considers the organisation of reading in the classroom one should remember that reading should not be regarded as a self-contained subject but rather as an integral part of the whole curriculum; success in reading engenders confidence and further success and, therefore, motivation is a very important factor (I have found that if a word has an intense meaning for a child then, generally, he will learn it quickly and recognise it easily); the teacher's faith and enthusiasm in the approach that she adopts is of utmost importance and her relationship with the child will have an effect on the child's progress in reading; fairly frequent short periods of reading are better than infrequent longer periods, and a lot of revision is required; every child should be allowed to proceed at his own rate and the teacher should adopt individual methods to help certain children overcome their own particular difficulties.

The way in which reading is organised in the classroom will depend on the organisation of the school and the classes and, particularly, the teacher's faith in the approach she wishes to adopt.

Class reading

This is an approach which has generally fallen into disuse. A set of books is given out to the class so that each child has the same book. The children read in turn and many stutter and stammer through their words and are completely unable to follow the readings of their colleagues. This approach did not take into consideration the fact that few children are likely to be at the same level of reading attainment.

Group reading

Grouping may help a teacher because it allows him to deal with a smaller range of reading ability within each respective group. The main reason for using group reading is because it assists the teacher in catering for the individual needs of his pupils. The size of reading groups should be flexible. Frequently the class is divided into groups of three to six, with the children having the same approximate reading age. One child is usually appointed as a leader and the reading is frequently from the same text. Unknown words are either 'worked out' by the group or the leader asks the teacher. The teacher moves from group to group and spends most of her time with those children who are experiencing difficulty. A teacher may find that a class divided up into three, four or five groups or more may suit her requirements, her own particular approach, class size, space, materials, etc.

A few teachers may arrange their reading groups and number them one, two, three, etc. Other teachers may use colours to differentiate the groups or may label the groups with the names of the group leaders. But it is ridiculous to attempt to arrange the reading groups so that the children do not know who the better readers are. Children quickly appreciate where and why they are placed in certain groups because they know the 'top readers', the 'poor readers' and those who 'come in between'.

A leader of a group may be a child whose reading attainment is well above that of the remainder of the group. Several different texts may be used in the same group.

Group reading has its advantages in that the children 'move on' without the direct supervision of the teacher. All members of the group are involved in either reading or listening. Members of the group work as a unit in that they share their knowledge.

There are, however, several disadvantages in using group reading. There can be disciplinary problems and a teacher can spend most of her time keeping the groups under control and in their correct places. There is a danger that if the group leader is a far better reader than the rest of the group, he may be held back. The varying interests and attainments of a small group may be quite substantial and so may the reading speeds. One child may struggle through his book whereas another loses patience because he wishes to move on more rapidly. Another factor, sometimes forgotten, is that reading aloud is frequently slower than silent reading. It is usually more advisable to use groups for other reading activities such as reading games and the use of reading apparatus.

Setting

In this approach a whole year group or maybe two or more groups combine for reading activities. The most able groups can be quite large and these usually concentrate on silent reading. The remainder of the children can be graded into progressively smaller groups, the smallest group consisting of those at the beginning stage of reading. The smaller groups can be concentrating on specific reading skills and promotion can be arranged so that children move on to other groups.

Individual reading

One is able to observe a wide range of reading ability in almost every classroom. Teachers quickly observe the many significant differences that exist among children, both in learning rate and in learning capacity. In one classroom there may be several children with an average level in vocabulary development, below average in comprehension and above average in word attack. These individual differences become more and more pronounced as children move up through the school. In one particular class of children, the range of reading ability may be about one-and-a-half years with each additional year of primary schooling. Some children will improve very quickly, sometimes gaining about two years in reading attainment for each year spent in school; whereas slower children will frequently do well to gain about half a year during the same period.

If a teacher is planning a reading programme with the individual requirements of each child in mind, then it should be remembered that growth in reading ability is never a smooth, upward curve. Children will differ in the speed with which they are able to complete various pieces of work.

Because of children's individual differences, some will require more practice than others in order to attain the desired proficiency. In an ideal teaching situation, each child would work with his own teacher who would teach a particular skill at the child's individual level. In practice, however, if a teacher is confronted with thirty to forty pupils, she finds it extremely difficult to provide sufficient time so that she is able to confer with all pupils on an individual basis even though this may always be her goal. This problem may be partially overcome, however, if material is so planned that pupils are allowed to progress in small, logical steps at their own pace and maximum learning may take place if the material provides the learner with an immediate indication of how he has performed. Children become frustrated if forced to conform to a pace that is either too slow or too fast. It is extremely important, therefore, that the teacher should keep detailed information on the progress of each individual child.

The aim of individualised reading is to allow each child to select reading material which interests him and, it is hoped that, motivated by interest and guided by the teacher, he will progress at his own individual rate of progress. There has to be careful recording of his selection of reading material and if his interest appears to be too narrow it may be necessary to provide material to widen his interest.

Programmed materials are important and useful because they allow the pupil to move on at his own particular pace. These materials can be found in three forms—material used in a teaching machine, material on separate cards and material in the form of a workbook or book. Stott's *Programmed Reading Kit* (Holmes McDougall) is useful programmed reading material with a phonic basis. *The SRA Reading Laboratories* provide a very good reading development programme.

Individualised reading, therefore, is an attempt to cater for the individual reading differences which are found in every classroom. This approach depends on the availability of an abundance of books and reading material for various levels of reading attainment. The child selects his own reading material and it is hoped that this will cater for his interests and help to maintain his motivation. It has been noticed that children appear to indulge in more reading when they are left to select their own reading material. The teacher attempts to spend some time with each child. The child reads to the teacher and this period is regarded as a time for teaching and carrying out diagnostic procedures. The whole approach creates a closer relationship between pupil and teacher. The better readers are not held back when this form of organisation is used. There is no need for a child to concentrate on one reading scheme. The system is regarded by many teachers as the only approach because a skill should be taught when a child shows his need for it.

The most valuable contribution to the teaching of reading is made when the teacher is in a position to give individual attention to the child. Teaching machines, tape recorders and other aids and media may cater to some extent for certain individuals, but they cannot replace the one-to-one relationship between teacher and child and the encouragement and support the teacher is able to give as a result of this one-to-one approach. It is at the beginning stage of reading that this personal contact is so very important. Eventually, when the child's reading ability increases, personal contact will become less, but the child should not be neglected at the beginning stage and the teacher must make every effort to hear children reading as often as possible. This is the finest teaching situation, when the crux of the child's reading problem may be fully appreciated. When a teacher listens to a child reading, he can ensure that the child has a feeling of success which he may not experience if left for too long on his own. The teacher's presence alone may increase a child's efforts. As a result of listening to the child, the teacher is in an ideal position to assess the child's progress and provide the necessary additional reading material required to increase the child's reading growth.

Ideally, the teacher should listen to children reading every day, but it is fully appreciated that this is virtually impossible with a class of between thirty and forty children. Even when a teacher attempts to listen to as many children as she can, she is naturally concerned about what the other children are doing. Games, activities, self-corrective materials, workbooks, teaching machines and other aids and media may be used to supplement the teacher's individual contact. These would also give the teacher the opportunity to attend to the poor readers who require more personal attention. If the teacher can find sufficient time just to listen to her children then she will be in a better position to fully appreciate any difficulties being experienced and attempt to assist these children by providing activities designed to overcome these difficulties.

It is advisable that one member of the staff of a school should specialise in the teaching of reading and take responsibility for organising and advising. It may be possible to have an 'adoption system' whereby each teacher adopts a poor reader whom he sees for ten minutes each day.

It is important that records are kept of a child's progress in reading. Frequently, the only record is a slip of cardboard recording the page reached by the child. This is not sufficient. A child's difficulties must be noted. Frequently, a teacher notes that a particular child is experiencing a certain difficulty. An attempt may be made at the time to assist the child, but then the difficulty may be forgotten by the teacher because on the next occasion the child does not encounter the difficulty in the particular text he is reading to the teacher. But the child is still experiencing difficulty with the original problem. (See a further discussion in Chapter 10—The Class Reading Programme.)

The classroom library

Reading books and other reading materials and equipment designed to develop specific stages in learning to read should not be the only reading material available in the classroom. There should be a supply of general books such as picture dictionaries, reference books and illustrated story books of various kinds. The prevailing learning and teaching situation in many primary schools gives rise to a situation where many questions and problems arise which need to be answered or solved.

The first essential must be the provision of adequate classroom libraries or book corners. These books should be meant for the children and should be freely available and not merely on display. There should be a carefully selected classroom collection of books and they should be near at hand so that children can use them with the minimum disruption. The situation should be such that the children can easily find the books which are best suited to their age and ability, and the younger or less able child is not faced with the problem of selecting a book from a larger group containing many books which are completely unsuitable for his own particular needs. Similarly, story books need to be changed when they have served their purpose and not at a specific time on a particular day.

The suitability of books for classes of children is very important and the teacher has to consider the length of the stories or the amount and depth of detail given, the extent of the vocabulary and, in the case of younger children, the size of print. A child unfortunate enough to encounter a high percentage of books which are unsuitable for any of these reasons might well have doubts about the usefulness and value of books and of his own ability to use them profitably. For many children their school days will be the only opportunity they will have to be in contact with books for any length of time. Their teachers must ensure that their impressions of books as media are favourable and a carefully chosen, graded classroom collection is the best way to do this.

The school library

Adequate classroom provision should be made first and this should be followed by a central school library. This central school library can supplement the classroom libraries in several ways:

a It can contain books which are too expensive to duplicate.

b It can provide a wider range of background books on specific subjects for which there is likely to be a demand because of the use of the project method.

c It can cater for children at both ends of the ability scale, e.g. the infant child with a reading age of 9+ years.

    d It can supply books for pleasure reading, suitable for each age range, which can be stored and exchanged with books in the classroom at convenient periods.

Until a suitable number of books can be purchased those available should be allowed to flow freely between classrooms so that the needs of the eight-year-old with a reading age of 11 + years can be satisfied.

If books are to be a natural part of the environment of the school, these books must be good books. The selection of books is an important task of every teacher. If teachers are to choose the books for their class libraries, there must be opportunities for them to see and examine what is available. This is not an easy task and there must be some kind of guidance to aid selection. Teachers can consult the following:

    a *Books for Young People (Group 1)* (Library Association).
    b *Four to Fourteen* by Kathleen Lines (National Book League, CUP).
    c *Primary School Library Books* (School Library Assoc.).
    d *Intent Upon Reading* by M. Fisher (Brockhampton Press).
    e *Tales out of School* by G. Trease (Heinemann Educational).
    f *The Use of Books* (Department of Education and Science).
    g *The School Library* (Department of Education and Science).
    h *Literature and the Young Child* by Joan Cass (Longmans).

Fiction of the right kind has a place of vital importance in children's development. It is the main field of imaginative literature which often has the strongest appeal to most children at certain stages in their development.

Most teachers realise that recreational books can provide the source of much useful and purposeful activity in the primary school. Creative writing can often be inspired by a story, a poem, a character or an incident, while an historical novel, particularly if its origins are local, can lead to environmental studies but, primarily, the child reads for sheer delight or pleasure.

Chapter 7

Factors associated with reading disability

The nature of reading ability is very complex and the results of many investigations into reading disabilities emphasise that it is only very rarely that reading difficulties can be attributed to a single factor. Usually it is a question of a whole complex of factors which can be regarded as being simultaneously connected with reading difficulties, though the degree of the relationship may vary.

The complex character of the reading process makes it very difficult to survey the causes of reading difficulties and, as a result, educationists are still faced with a number of problems. It is frequently only possible to state that certain factors are connected with reading difficulties. It has been found that factors or groups of factors are apparently related to reading difficulties but it has not always been possible to differentiate between cause and effect. Previous investigations have shown that children who are labelled as being seriously backward or retarded in reading may exhibit many anomalies, that is, physical, mental, social and emotional deficiencies, but research has shown that many of the anomalies exhibited have little or no relation to reading failure in *certain individual cases,* but are of *significant importance in others.* These investigations have emphasised that great care must be taken in reaching conclusions concerning the specific causes of reading disability.

Intellectual factors

Poor intellectual capacity will inevitably retard the progress of reading ability, and the child with low intellectual capacity may well have difficulty in reasoning out the systematic relationship between word shapes and word sounds and all the other intricacies. Generally speaking, the correlation between success in reading and the intelligence quotient is fairly high. However, if verbal intelligence tests are used the correlation is artificially raised because of the poor ability of the backward readers. Usually children with a low degree of intelligence differ from those of normal intelligence in their slower pace of learning to read. These children require a larger period of pre-reading activities and a slower rate of teaching. However, one should remember that there is a danger that if we attribute reading failure to low intelligence as the basic common cause, some teachers may classify children as dull because they are poor readers. Many children of normal intelligence are retarded in reading. Houghton and Daniels (1966) have shown that children regarded as ineducable on the basis of their low IQ could learn to read. Vernon (1957) warned of the danger of attributing reading failure to low intelligence as the basic cause:

'It may be claimed that whenever the measured IQ of cases of reading disability is not subnormal, there can be no deficiency in the reasoning process. But intelligence tests as a rule cover only certain types of reasoning. It may be that these are not closely related to the complex reasoning processes which must be employed in learning to read. In particular, they do not cover the processes of grasping the systematic arrangement in correct order which is so essential in reading.'

The relationship between intelligence and reading ability is not such that a prediction based only on intelligence test scores can be made with a high degree of certainty as to the development of reading ability. On the other hand, the relationship is of such significance that intelligence must be regarded as an important factor in the development of reading ability.

Poor language development

It is generally agreed that a child requires a good vocabulary and a competent use of language before he can learn to read. Thus backwardness in language development may lead to failure in reading. Teachers must appreciate the relationship between language development and the child's ability in beginning reading. This point has been particularly stressed by Thackray (1965).

We all appreciate that infants coming from homes that are intellectually and culturally adequate are able to acquire language efficiency quite incidentally. We also appreciate that children coming from culturally deprived homes and the intellectually slow are not so fortunate. The work of many investigators has brought about a greater interest in the study of language development and its influence on the child's ability to read effectively. (Luria, 1961; Williams, 1961; Lewis, 1963; Morris, 1966; Kellmer-Pringle, 1966; Goodacre, 1967; Lewis, 1969 and Gulliford, 1969.)

At this juncture it is necessary to give two definitions for the term 'speech'. Speech can be defined as: (a) the ability to articulate; or (b) a speaking vocabulary.

Thus speech difficulties might imply: (a) articulatory disorders, e.g. stuttering, or; (b) the inability to express ideas clearly and paucity of meaningful language experience.

Articulatory disorders

Speech defects can be due to physical causes. The mouth, palate and teeth may be deformed. Occasionally the cause may be an emotional one and this may give rise to lisping and stammering. These defects can frequently affect the child's powers of discrimination and his attempts at phonic analysis. Therefore inaccurate articulation may directly affect reading by creating a confusion in the sounds of words to be associated with the printed symbols. Malmquist (1958) found there was a tendency for 'poor' readers to have a higher frequency of speech defects during pre-school age than in the case of 'medium' or 'good' readers. Reed (1966) has produced evidence to suggest that there is a pronounced association between auditory high frequency weakness and retardation or distortion in the understanding and articulation of speech and gross retardation in reading skills and written expression.

A poor speaking vocabulary

Reading develops from speech and it can be dangerous to force young children during the initial stages of learning to read if there have not been sufficient activities to create what Schonell

113

called, many years ago, 'a functional language' beforehand. There is a danger that children may be forced into reading before they have developed vocabularies to express their own ideas clearly. It is now generally accepted that children should have developed an ability for oral expression before they can be expected to read and comprehend the ideas of others.

It is generally recognised that socio-economic factors greatly influence language development. Socio-economic background is reflected in all phases of the child's development and this is more marked in language than in other aspects of development. Environments lacking adequate stimulation also limit the child's progress through the language limitations of his parents. Where parents are less gifted and experienced linguistically, the child does not profit from the opportunity of developing by imitation. Kellmer-Pringle (1966) has emphasised that the most important period for the fostering of language and speech is during pre-school years. The influence of the home environment is brought out in the work of Battin and Haugh (1964). Their book may be regarded as a practical manual for parents.

Physical factors

Generally speaking, there appear to be two ways in which reading ability can be affected by physical defects. Firstly, children often appear to tire quickly, become inattentive and lack concentration when their constitutions have been lowered as a result of illness or other physical defects. Secondly, this situation may lead to prolonged illness and absence from school. Frequently, the physical condition that interferes with educational progress consists not of grave or well-defined diseases, but of milder, vaguer and more generalised conditions that sap the child's physical strength and so weaken his mental powers. There is a view propounded by several investigators including Rabino-vitch (in Money, 1962), Bowlby (1965) and Stott (1966), that some physical defects can arise from harmful changes in the environment before and during the birth of the child.

Auditory factors

Defective hearing can impose a very serious obstacle to learning. A child suffering from defective hearing may miss much of what the teacher is saying and so he finds his work difficult. The auditory abilities involved in learning to read are:

a Auditory perception—the ability to be aware of sounds.
b Auditory memory—the ability to remember a sound which has previously been perceived.
c Auditory discrimination—the ability to appreciate differences and similarities in sounds.

It should be quite apparent that learning to read must be exceptionally difficult for the deaf child even though one appreciates that deaf and mute children do learn to read, but usually only when special help is given. Frequently, slight hearing loss goes unnoticed. Luria (1961) has stated that if, through a deficiency of any sort, language does not develop then other processes will also be retarded. Reed (1966) has produced evidence to suggest a pronounced association between auditory high frequency weakness and retardation or distortion in the understanding and articulation of speech, and immature language development, including gross retardation in reading skills.

Auditory discrimination

When a child begins to associate sounds with objects and does not confuse certain sounds that are similar, such as Tommy and tummy, Tony and tunnel, then he is beginning to master auditory discrimination. If a child is eventually to tackle phonic work then he will require the skill of auditory discrimination. If he is to 'unlock' a word which he has not met before, it will be necessary for him to appreciate that a word has its own sound pattern, that this pattern may be broken down into a series of sounds which are arranged in a definite sequence, and that these sounds relate to the shapes of letters or a combination of such shapes.

Some children who have been diagnosed as having poor auditory discrimination have in fact been suffering from hearing loss. On the other hand, a child may have adequate hearing but he may experience difficulty in appreciating the differences between the sounds of letters. A child may have a short auditory memory span and his undifferentiated auditory discrimination interferes with the interpretation of what he hears. If a child is unable to discriminate between the beginning sounds of such words as 'tap' and 'sat', or if he does not appreciate the difference

115

between the vowel sounds of 'a' and 'e' in such words as 'pet' and 'pat', he will find it extremely difficult to learn to read, especially if the method used requires him to associate sounds with letters.

Visual factors

Defective vision may affect a child's ability to learn to read because it may cause such a degree of discomfort that the actual process of reading creates eye strain and fatigue. The visual abilities involved in learning are:

    a Visual perception—the ability to be aware of an image.

    b Visual memory—the ability to recall a visual image.

    c Visual discrimination—the ability to appreciate differences and similarities in shape, size and colour.

    d Left/right orientation—the ability to read a line of print from left to right.

Children exhibiting reading difficulties may suffer from near-sightedness, far-sightedness, astigmatism and various forms of eye muscle imbalance. A near-sighted child may be able to see well at close range but may not be able to see what is written on the blackboard or see the print on labels and wall charts. The far-sighted child shows no difficulty in seeing print or objects at a distance but has difficulty in reading print at close range. Astigmatism frequently affects clearness of perception. A child suffering from eye muscle imbalance may not be able to receive a single image as he focuses on a printed page.

It is extremely important that primary skills are well-developed before a child starts reading, in order that the habits of regular, rhythmic, horizontal eye movements can be established. (There is a collection of authoritative opinion in the work edited by Money, 1962.) The child who is pushed into reading before he has these controls may develop tensions and faulty eye habits.

Visual discrimination

    'There is a great deal of evidence revealing the importance of visual perceptual skills in early school success. The association with reading is strong, particularly in the early stages of reading where children are primarily learning to discriminate differences in letter and word shapes.'

                                               (Krausen, R. 1972).

116

In order to read efficiently a child must be able to recognise printed symbols instantly. Certain symbols differ only in minute details. Certain letters are almost identical except that they face in different directions, such as 'b' and 'd', 'b' and 'p', 'u' and 'n' and 'p' and 'q'. Therefore, if a child suffers from poor visual discrimination, he will have difficulty in recognising words, particularly if these words have similar configurations such as 'pant' and 'punt', 'want' and 'went', and 'when' and 'then'. Such a child may continue to misread, substitute, add or omit words. Thackray (1965) found that when relating various measures of readiness at five years to eventual progress in reading, there was a considerable relationship with measures of visual and auditory discrimination.

Specific training in the skills of visual perception, analysis and synthesis should be used with those children suffering from visual defects and similar training for those with auditory defects. Johnson and Myklebust (1967) have placed particular emphasis on such training. A detailed discussion of the perceptual abilities seen as important in learning to read can be found in Tansley (1967). Those discussed include hand/eye co-ordination, visual rhythm, visual sequencing, auditory discrimination, auditory rhythm, visual discrimination and form appreciation.

Left/right orientation

It is very important that during the beginning stage of reading children learn that the eyes move from left to right across the page. The majority of children learn the correct sequences without difficulty through incidental learning, through activities involved in play and bodily activities. This may be the reason why teachers neglect this very essential skill. Some children come to school needing specific practice in this skill before making an attempt at reading. They may have poor perceptual attack. They may begin at the right-hand side of the page, or may begin in the middle of a word and move either to left or right missing out the initial letter of the word. Children with problems concerning direction and/or spatial orientation may have difficulty distinguishing between 'was' and 'saw' and 'on' and 'no'. They may also reverse letters in writing, reading or speaking. For example, these children may write 'flim' for 'film', read 'three' for 'there' or say 'emeny' for 'enemy'. The skill of left/right orientation must never be taken for granted by the teacher

117

because if it is not mastered then a child may exhibit harmfu
reading habits including omissions, reversals, missing lines, etc

Left-handedness

Left-handedness need not in itself be a handicap to reading, bu
the physical act involved in writing with the left hand can give
rise to untidy work and an impaired visual feedback from the
writing. Clark (1957) has suggested that because of the pushing
action of the left-handed child during writing, early work is
inclined to be dirty and untidy because of the smearing caused by
the hand passing over the writing. Another unfortunate effect
however, is that the left-handed child tends to obscure the
series of letters he is writing, his hand and pencil moving over the
word as he is writing. As a result the visual feedback which he
gets from the word, as he writes it, is impaired.

Emotional and personality factors

Emotional and personality problems might be the *cause* o:
reading failure. Stott (1958) carried out surveys covering ap
proximately 1,000 children. The children's adjustment was
assessed on his Bristol Social Adjustment Guides and he found
that maladjustment was greater with the more backward child
Morris (1966) found that poor readers exhibited more signs o:
maladjustment when assessed by Stott's Bristol Social Adjust
ment Guides than did good readers. (But not all maladjusted
children are backward in reading and not all reading failure:
are maladjusted.) The severe maladjustments of the extremely
neurotic child are very obvious; but the minor adjustments
which a child must make when he enters school are so many
that he may not be able to apply himself to reading. A child
who experiences emotional upsets as he is growing up may face
the school with considerable anxiety. The resulting disturbance
can be so overwhelming that he learns very little. Much
emphasis has been placed on the adverse effects of parenta
behaviour and school conditions.

A new trend of thought emphasises the effect of adverse con
ditions prevailing during pregnancy or during birth. Stott (1966

118

has suggested that because the part of the brain which controls behaviour develops towards the end of pregnancy, any damage just before or during birth may be the cause of emotional and personality maladjustment, delinquency, inability to concentrate, temper tantrums and enuresis. Bowlby (1965) has put forward similar views.

There does not appear to be any doubt that maladjustment can be the *effect* of reading failure. Reading failure can lead to frustration, disinterest, discouragement and other conditions. Emotional and personality problems can also be both the *cause* and *effect* of reading disability. (Sampson, in 1966, provided an excellent review of the professional literature on reading and adjustment.) A survey of remedial services carried out by Sampson (1969) showed that many remedial teachers emphasised how important it was to be aware of emotional and personality factors in their work.

Home background

There is considerable evidence that poverty of environmental stimulation at an early age can result in a stunting of the learning process which is possibly irretrievable, and which may not be compensated for by the later placing of a child in an enriched environment. Lack of culture in the home may retard the acquisition of language. Children have less experience with books and may not fully appreciate what reading really is and so have less interest in acquiring it. Many surveys show a lower average reading achievement and a higher incidence of backwardness among children with lower socio-economic status than with those of higher socio-economic status. (Morris, 1966; Kellmer-Pringle, 1966; Goodacre, 1967.)

Recent research into home background has been inclined to be more systematic in as far as attempts have been made to distinguish, in more detail, those aspects which appear to influence reading ability. These aspects are (a) cultural, (b) material and economic, (c) motivational, and (d) emotional.

Cultural factors

I would suggest that, while poor economic background is reflected in all aspects of the child's development, cultural deprivation has a very marked effect. This is most marked in language development. Irrespective of intelligence and other factors, maximum language development is dependent upon an adequate environmental stimulation. Where the standard of English is low, where books are few and where conversation is limited in extent and variety, it is only to be expected that the standard of English is meagre and there is no inclination for many children to express themselves fluently and correctly.

Material and economic factors

In many of our large cities and in many towns where sometimes it is least expected, there exist appalling housing conditions which make it very difficult for the tenants to maintain the standards of decency, morality and health which are necessary to stabilise home life. Many people living in these areas are in the lower income group or have sustained some social tragedy. The conditions of some problem families are often reached by a slow process of devolution in which the relative unconcern of responsible authorities and the ostracism of neighbours play a part.

In the past, socio-economic status was frequently defined according to the father's occupation and income. Today, however, it is becoming clear that this does not distinguish the living standards of people as well as it used to. It is now necessary to use an index which reflects housing conditions since these vary widely within various occupation classes.

Motivational factors

Indifference to education on the part of the parents is becoming an increasing problem. There is a section of the community which has pursued a policy of failing to give its children sufficient direction in the selective choice of work after school. They regard the high wages and relatively unskilled work as quite sufficient for the child, and, as a result, they do not have any interest in the education of their children. Children are great imitators and they very quickly adopt the values and ideals of their parents. Children of two years and older have a tendency to act in a number of ways like their parents. They adopt parental mannerisms, play parental roles and incorporate in their own value systems many of the values, restrictions and ideals of their parents. Therefore, in a very short time lack of parental encouragement can adversely influence the child and his approach to school work.

120

Emotional factors

There are several elements which are receiving greater recognition as contributory factors in reading disability. These are un- favourable emotional relationships, such as ambivalence, rejection of the child by the parent, marital discord, absence of a parent, and sibling rivalry. It has frequently been suggested that a 'broken home' is a home where the child does not live together with both his real parents but, probably, a better definition should place more emphasis on the separation of parents in their love and understanding of each other. It must also be remembered that a child can be deprived, even though he is living at home, if his mother is unable to give him the necessary loving care.

It must be noted, however, that many children learn to read, and read well, even though they may be surrounded by many adverse environmental influences. But a child from a poor, overcrowded, emotionally unstable and uncultural home may be less interested in learning to read because he receives very little encouragement from his home environment.

School conditions

When one considers that the school is the place where reading is usually learned, a logical assumption could be that an important cause of reading failure would show itself in the school. There is no doubt that the approach of the school concerning methods of teaching, teaching materials, promotion, and flexibility in adapting materials to individual children will influence the progress of individual children. The personality of the teacher, the size of the class and many other factors can be considered as possible causes of reading failure.

Inefficient teaching methods can impede progress in reading and this inefficiency can actually develop the growth of undesir- able habits in reading. There is no doubt that some children will not respond to methods which are suited to the rest of the class. In many schools there is a need for more teachers to have:

a a far better understanding of individual differences,
b more knowledge of what is actually involved in the process of reading,
c more flexibility in the methods of teaching reading,
d more knowledge of developmental reading and its

application to individual children,

e more knowledge of early ascertainment procedures for children with learning difficulties and the use of diagnostic materials,

f more knowledge of teaching aids, reading materials and other reading media,

g more detailed records and follow-up procedures for those children experiencing reading difficulty,

h the knowledge that most children at some time in their early school life have a strong interest in learning to read, and that this interest decreases unless the teacher ensures that every child makes some progress, and that the child knows that he is making progress, however small.

(Untimely promotion) can have an adverse effect on a child's reading progress. Amongst backward readers one may find some who have been promoted too quickly, some too slowly, and others who have been promoted from an infant school run on 'progressive' lines, with an abundance of freedom and directed play, to a junior school that still adopts a 'formal' and stricter approach. This sudden change can have a detrimental effect on the child. What makes matters worse, in certain areas, is that there is little or no liaison between the infant and the junior school. The junior school may have limited or no knowledge of a child's ability or difficulties in reading.

Morris (1966) has emphasised that, in general, backward readers have had poorer school facilities and supplies of reading materials. The schools attended by good readers were better organised by the head teachers. During her Kent survey she found that, although nearly half the children who entered the junior school were still in the early stages of learning to read, among the teachers of these children 75 per cent had received no training in infant teaching methods and 52 per cent had no experience in an infant school nor *knew how to teach the initial stages of reading*. However, Goodacre (1967b) has suggested that, in general, infant teachers are better trained. Collins (1961) stated that the most obvious cause of retardation is bad teaching environments or generally inadequate or inappropriate educational stimulation. He also stated that 'more slow learning is due to bad teaching than is generally admitted'.

Many educationists have placed considerable emphasis on the different teaching methods and the resulting reading achievements

Morris (1966) found little difference in achievement between children taught by phonic and by other methods. But Chall (1967), after a very detailed study of a large number of schools, reached the conclusion that phonic methods were definitely superior. Hughes (1970), although emphasising the apparent neglect of phonic methods, stresses that the most important criterion involved in the teaching of reading is not so much the ✳ method being used, but rather the 'individual teacher's faith and enthusiasm in the method she is using'.

There is no doubt that a cause of reading failure can show itself in the school situation. Inefficient teaching, and all that this entails, and other adverse factors can have a detrimental effect on a child's reading progress. It can be argued, however, that many children learn to read in spite of adverse school circumstances; therefore we can conclude that there must be additional factors at work affecting the child experiencing reading difficulty.

+ what a child is going to read

Chapter 8

Specific dyslexia

Reading skill is a complex of abilities and includes visual perception, visual memory and visual discrimination; auditory perception, auditory memory and auditory discrimination; association of visual and auditory material; linguistic ability and a capacity for the detailed analysis of the sound structure of individual words.

The difficulty in relating reading failure to one condition or a culmination of conditions has given rise to the concept of a *specific disability*. The term 'dyslexia' is coming into use to describe children with severe reading difficulties. *Dyslexia* by itself means impairment of the ability to comprehend and interpret the written word, but the terms *word blindness, congenital word blindness, specific reading disability, specific developmental dyslexia, specific dyslexia* and *dyslexia* are all used to describe children who fail to learn to read. This variety of terms arises from the fact that attempts to identify what the children are suffering from have not led to uniform conclusions. A few educationists use the term 'dyslexia' to describe all backward readers. Others use the term for children of average or above average intelligence who are severely backward in reading and who are not suffering from defective vision, defective hearing, high absenteeism, poor home backgrounds and severe emotional problems. A tremendous amount of misunderstanding has arisen from the use and interpretation of these different terms. Reid (1968) says that the controversy is partly a problem of communication.

Critchley (1964) discusses the early studies of 'word-blindness' and refers to an article in the Lancet in 1895 by James Hinshelwood, a Glasgow eye specialist, who refers to a case of 'word-blindness'. Since this time there have been conflicting opinions regarding this disability as a cause of failure to learn to read.

124

There are examples of adults with known brain injury who have lost the ability to read. However, in some cases, other areas of the brain may take over the functions of the damaged area.

It has been suggested that if we use the adjective 'specific', then 'specific dyslexia' should be defined as the failure to learn to read despite conventional instruction, a culturally adequate home, proper motivation, intact senses, normal intelligence and *freedom from neurological defects*. It is also frequently suggested that a child suffering from specific dyslexia suffers from *word-blindness*—an inability to perceive written symbols and relate them to specific sounds. At the same time it is emphasised that this condition should not be confused with 'non-dyslexic' backwardness in reading which may be caused by low intelligence, defective vision or hearing, *serious neurological brain damage*, inadequate teaching, absenteeism and emotional disturbance as a result of a disrupted home or parental anxiety.

Doctors tend to use a diagnostic term—'dyslexia' or 'word-blindness', but most educational psychologists do not consider that a specific condition has been identified. The views of psychologists have been affected by certain children having been labelled as 'dyslexic' simply because they were backward readers, and particularly because many of these backward readers eventually learnt to read quite efficiently. Therefore, many teachers and educational psychologists do not accept the existence of specific dyslexia, but there are certain educational psychologists, paediatricians and neurologists who have no doubts that specific dyslexia is a *primary disorder*—although they all state that no one method of diagnosis or remedial treatment can cater for the needs of every dyslexic case.

Attempts have been made to isolate those children with specific dyslexia. A survey was carried out in the Isle of Wight by Professor Tizard (1965) and he claimed that 1·5 per cent of the schoolchildren suffered from specific dyslexia. There have been claims of between 10 and 15 per cent in the USA and Scandinavia. But Dr Morris (1966) during her Kent survey found no evidence to suggest that such a condition existed. Her findings agreed with those of Malmquist (1959).

What causes specific dyslexia? Answers are highly controversial. Ingram (1960) states that many children classified as dyslexics suffer from visuo-spatial difficulties—involving the recognition and/or the writing of printed symbols; correlating and synthesising difficulties—relating symbols to their sounds and combining words from their components; and difficulties in language comprehension and expression. Lovell (1964) suggests that the failure of many backward readers is associated with, though not necessarily caused by, a cluster of factors such as poor auditory-visual integration, spatial orientation and motor performance.

It has been suggested that the defect may arise from slow maturation in the development of the functions of the brain (Critchley, 1964). It has also been suggested that the cause is some disfunction of the brain due to damage during pregnancy or at birth (Kawi and Pasamanick, 1959; Prechtl, 1962; Stott, 1966). But others have suggested that quite a number of these children do not suffer from irreparable brain damage but rather from slow maturation of the neurological mechanisms (Birch, 1962), and that many children outgrow their difficulties by the time they are nine or ten years old (Benton, 1962). It is a known fact that some children suffering from brain damage which has affected their perceptual processes do eventually learn to read. But Clark (1970) emphasises that the controversy should not be about the various cases of identified gross brain damage, 'but rather the extension of this concept to a developmental one, where a child has failed to acquire the ability to read and spell in the *absence of gross neurological impairment*'. (My italics.)

Tests used for the diagnosis of specific dyslexia indicate that there is no one syndrome. If a child exhibits one of its many features this does not mean that he definitely has specific dyslexia. Many children may have a collection of symptoms, but the significance of the presence of some of these symptoms depends upon the age of the child. After all, many are found at certain ages in children who are normal readers.

At the Word Blind Centre in London (no longer operating) children arrive with similar patterns. They are growing up normally in every way except that when their contemporaries are starting to read and learning to spell these children lag behind. Some of the children can read, but can't spell; others can spell and write but can't read. The personnel at the Word Blind Centre are convinced that dyslexia is a specific disability probably based on some sort of perceptual weakness, probably formed by neurological brain damage. But there are similar types of perceptual difficulties which affect the identity of the disorder.

Tests used at the Centre for diagnosis indicate that there is no one syndrome. Some children have visuo-spatial difficulties. Their writing is usually untidy with uneven characters, often reversed, rotated or omitted, and contains some very fundamental mis-spellings. Typical errors are the writing of 'fo' for 'of', or 'not' as 'tno'. Similar letters such as 'b' and 'd', and 'm' and 'w' may be confused, and sometimes the writing takes on such bizarre characteristics as the fusion of two consecutive letters. Some dyslexics may have a linguistic defect because of a perceptible hearing 'blind spot'. These children may have speech difficulty. They often make mistakes when distinguishing between the sounds 'v' and 'th' as well as when writing them down.

Word games, jigsaws, various visual and auditory discrimination programmes, picture naming, and many other kinds of perceptual training exercises form the basis of the teaching. If a child is weak in visuo-spatial perception he might be helped by paying particular attention to the acoustic properties of words and associating them with the kinaesthetic—tactile aspects of writing. Sometimes a child is encouraged to write each letter in sand in order to get the feel of the letter. A typewriter might also be used. Those children with problems of auditory discrimination, poor recall of the visual symbols for sounds, or sequencing difficulties, are helped by programmed reading aids. In Stott's Programmed Reading Kit, sounds are introduced as they are heard, not as separate, isolated units. Many of the aids used can be played in the form of games.

I have concluded that the symptoms used to determine whether some children suffer from specific dyslexia include the following:

i Many of these children are intelligent, physically and emotionally normal and, to begin with, they want to learn to read.

ii Many children are slow in beginning to talk and in mastering speech. They speak indistinctly and are slow to learn grammar—misusing prepositions and tenses. (The age of the child is very important here. One can expect six-year-olds to say, 'Mummy *gived* me a biscuit', or 'I *sleeped* with Daddy'.)

iii Children have difficulty in making others understand what they want to express. They have difficulty in understanding what is said to them. There is difficulty in following directions and in remembering a series of instructions.

iv There may be hereditary defects where reading disability is exhibited in other memebers of the family. (But parents who did not themselves read early and with enjoyment or who have had language difficulties, may not provide an environment which would stimulate children.)

v   Some children misread words in a text but proceed to give intelligent answers when asked questions based on the text. (It appears that the child is not reading the words 'incorrectly', but reading them as he sees them or making guesses based on his comprehension of the context or some part of the word which he feels familiar with.)

vi   Letters are written the wrong way round, or upside down. (This does not normally occur after eight years of age.) There is difficulty in reading certain letters. Those which are similar to one another, e.g. b–d, v–u, u–n, m–n, etc. Sounds which are similar, e.g. p–b, v–f, g–k, v–th, etc. There are reversals of words such as was–saw and no–on. (It should be remembered that reversals, additions and omissions of letters and words are fairly common errors when children are learning to read.)

vii   Some children have difficulty in appreciating direction and right from left (Benton, 1959; Belmont and Birch, 1965). They confuse left/right shoes, to/past on a clock face and page directions when handling a book. (Children do not usually appreciate right from left until they are between six and seven years old and, to begin with, only their own right and left. Right and left on others develops later.)

viii   Some children have ambilaterality. They have left-eyed, right-handed and left-footed dominance. (Zangwill, 1960).

ix   Certain children may be rather clumsy or awkward in their movements and have difficulty in copying geometric shapes. Their writing may be very poor and vowels are often omitted. Words are frequently scratched out and altered because of the child's indecision about spelling. The spelling may be quite bizarre with the writing having no relationship to the sounds of the words. The child may often use mirror writing.

Although considered separately, all these features are found to be associated with reading disability. However, most of them are only found to be so associated in a minority of cases, and the incidence of some of them does not differ to any significant extent from that found in the normal child population. When evaluating the concept of specific dyslexia, these features do not appear to cluster in any significant way.

No one has yet devised a foolproof method of diagnosing specific dyslexia. No one has yet uncovered a group of signs that are exclusive to the syndrome of specific dyslexia and are not found in other conditions of reading disability. It appears that the term 'specific dyslexia' is used to describe a case for which no particular cause of difficulty can be found.

A Report of the Advisory Committee on Handicapped Children (*Children with Specific Reading Difficulties*, 1972) states that the term 'dyslexia' has been very loosely used in educational contexts, and it is suggested that the term cannot be usefully employed for educational purposes. The Report refers to the use of the term 'acute dyslexia' used in Section 27 of the Chronically Sick and Disabled Persons Act, 1970, and it is suggested that the reading difficulties to which the Act intended to refer are 'not acute in the medical sense of coming sharply to a crisis; if, on the other hand, 'acute' is meant in the lay sense of severe, the Act omits to define the degree of severity'. The Advisory Committee prefer the use of the term 'specific reading difficulties' to describe the small group of children whose reading abilities (and perhaps writing, spelling and number abilities) are significantly below the standards which their abilities in other spheres would lead one to expect. It is further suggested that the educational needs of these children are part of the wider problem of reading backwardness of all kinds and that the 'very great majority of such children' will in time respond to good remedial teaching if this is closely geared to their individual needs.

The Advisory Committee take the view that there is a continuum spanning the whole range of reading abilities from those of the most fluent readers to those with the most severe difficulties. This continuum not only includes children whose reading abilities are significantly below the standards which their general abilities in other spheres would lead one to expect but also those children whose backwardness in reading is only one aspect of their overall backwardness. It is stressed that there is a danger that attention may be given to a group of children assessed as 'dyslexic' to the disadvantage of other children 'with perhaps equally severe difficulties but who happened not to be assessed'.

The Committee are highly sceptical of the view that a syndrome of 'developmental dyslexia' with a specific underlying cause and specific symptoms has been identified. It is also suggested that systematic screening of all children should take place at the end of the infant stage and not at the age of five years because this is too early a stage at which to attempt to identify children who are likely to have reading disabilities. I would disagree that screening should not take place earlier than seven or eight years. My many observations of infant children and conversations with infant teachers have convinced me that many children who are experiencing or who are going to experience reading difficulty can be 'spotted' at quite an early age in the infant school.

Chapter 9

Assessment of reading ability: some common difficulties and treatment

Because reading difficulty can only rarely be attributed to a single factor, the assessment of a child's reading failure must include a study of his overall physical and psychological development and the possible effects of many factors such as low intelligence, emotional and personality problems, poor language development, physical defects, poor home background, absenteeism and poor school conditions. (See assessment sheet used for 'Readiness for the beginning stages of reading' on page 151.)

The correlation between success in reading and intelligence is usually found to be quite high. Generally speaking, children with low intelligence read at a slower pace. But we must be aware of the danger of attributing reading failure to low intelligence as the basic cause. We may be tempted to label children as dull just because they are poor readers. There are many children of normal intelligence who are retarded in reading. A useful non-verbal intelligence test is the *Deeside Picture Test* (Harrap); this can be used with children aged between 5 and 7 years of age.

The child's vocabulary can be tested by using one of several published vocabulary tests:

    a *The Crichton Vocabulary Scale* for children of 10 years or below, (H. K. Lewis & Co.);

    b *The English Picture Vocabulary Test* (NFER);

    c Tests in Watts' *Language and Mental Development of Children,* (Harrap).

The following visual and auditory abilities should be assessed:

    a Visual perception—the ability to be aware of an image;

    b Visual discrimination—the ability to appreciate differences and similarities in shape, size and colour;

    c   Visual memory—the ability to recall a visual image;

    d   Left/right orientation—the ability to read a line of print from left to right;

    e   Auditory perception—the ability to be aware of sounds;

    f   Auditory discrimination—the ability to appreciate differences and similarities in sounds;

    g   Auditory memory—the ability to remember a sound which has previously been perceived.

The following tests may be useful for assessing the above abilities:

1   Daniels and Diack's *Standard Reading Tests* (Chatto & Windus). This is a battery of tests consisting of both attainment and diagnostic tests.

        Test 2   Copying abstract figures
             3   Copying a sentence
             4   Visual discrimination and orientation
           .5   Letter recognition
             6   Aural discrimination test

2   Wepman's *Auditory Discrimination Test* (Language Research Associates, Chicago).

3   *Marianne Frostig Development Test of Visual Perception* (available from NFER). There are five sub-tests:

           1   Eye-motor co-ordination
           2   Figure ground discrimination
           3   Form constancy
           4   Position in space
           5   Spatial relation

4   Further suggestions for tests and exercises may be found in:

    a   Tansley's *Reading and Remedial Reading* (Routledge & Kegan Paul).

    b   Moyle's *The Teaching of Reading* (Ward Lock Educational).

    c   Hughes' *Aids to Reading* (Evans Brothers).

    d   Hughes' *Phonics and the Teaching of Reading* (Evans Brothers).

    e   Jones' *From Left to Right* (Autobates Learning System Ltd.).

A simple speech test

It should be remembered that infant children have not completed their normal speech development and the teacher must consider what is regarded as normal for a particular age and what is a real speech defect. One should consider local pronunciations and the variations of articulation for a particular sound.

The following consonants and vowel sounds cover the main sounds used in English speech. The teacher may test the child's ability to articulate these sounds by saying the word and asking the child to repeat it, or by saying the word in a sentence and asking the child to repeat the sentence.

Consonants	**Vowels**
b — bed	a — rain
ch — chair	a — cat
d — dog	a — father
f — farm	a — above
g — gate	a — ball
h — house	e — bee
j — jump	e — wet
k — king	i — pie
l — like	i — sit
m — man	o — old
n — not	o — top
ng — sing	oo — food
p — pat	oo — look
r — run	u — use
s — see	u — up
sh — ship	
t — toys	
th — thing	
th — that	
v — van	
w — water	
wh — wheel	
y — yard	
z — zoo	

Phonic ability

Is the child able to:
a appreciate rhyme?
b discriminate between the initial sounds of words?
c blend sounds?
d recognise in print each letter that makes the sound?

Tests of phonic readiness and skills and further suggestions may be found in:
a Tansley's *Reading and Remedial Reading*.
b Hughes' *Phonics and the Teaching of Reading*.
c *The Swansea Test of Phonic Skills* (Blackwell).
d Jackson's *Get Reading Right* (Gibson), The Phonic Skills (PS) Tests.
e Bragg's *Test of Phonic Readiness* in *Special Education* Vol. L1, 2, 1962 and Tansley's *Reading and Remedial Reading*.
f See 'Assessing Phonic Skills' at the end of the chapter.

Reading tests

Word recognition tests

a Burt's *Graded Word Reading Test* (ULP), RA 4–15 years.
b Schonell's *Graded Word Reading Test* (Oliver & Boyd), RA 5–15 years.
c Vernon's *Graded Word Reading Test* (ULP), RA 5–18 years.

These are individual tests which reveal the child's ability to recognise a word without the aid of contextual clues. The reading age is found as follows:

$$\frac{\text{No. of words read correctly}}{10} + 5 \text{ years (4 years for Burt's)}$$
$$= \text{RA}$$

Sentence and prose reading tests

a Watts' *Holborn Reading Scale* (Harrup), RA 6–14 years.
b Daniels & Diack's *Standard Reading Test* (Chatto & Windus), RA 5 : 2–9 years.
c Neale's *Analysis of Reading Ability* (Macmillan), RA 6–14 years.

d   Wiseman & Wrigley's *Manchester Reading Comprehension Test* (ULP), RA 13 : 6–15 : 2.

e   Watts' NFER *Reading Test AD* (Ginn), RA 7 : 6–11 : 1 years. Also *Reading Test A, Reading Test BD.*

f   Barnard's NFER *Reading Comprehension Test DE* (Ginn), RA 10–12 years.

g   Bate's NFER *Secondary Reading Tests* 1, 2, 3 (Ginn), RA 11–15 years.
Also EH 1–3 Comprehension, EH 1–3 Vocabulary.

h   Schonell's *Diagnostic Reading Tests* (Oliver & Boyd).

i   Schonell's *Diagnostic and Attainment Tests* (Oliver & Boyd).

The Holborn Reading Scale and Neale's *Analysis of Reading Ability* are tests more related to a natural reading situation. The *Neale Analysis of Reading Ability* consists of short stories increasing in difficulty. Each story has a full page illustration. This test not only calculates an age for reading accuracy, but also speed of reading and comprehension. A form is used with the test for recording responses and this serves as a useful diagnostic record.

Group reading tests
(These are useful for a reading survey and to isolate those children with well-above average and well-below average reading attainments.)

a   Southgate's *Group Reading Tests V* (ULP), *Word Selection Test 1,* RA 5 : 9–7 : 9 years.
This assesses word recognition and takes about 15 minutes to administer.
Sentence Completion Test 2, RA 7–9 : 7 years.
This contains tests of comprehension and takes about 15 minutes.

b   Spooncer's *Group Reading Assessment* (ULP), RA 6 : 3–11 : 7 years.
This contains tests of word recognition and comprehension and takes about 15 minutes.

c   Watts' *Sentence Reading Test* (NFER), RA $7\frac{1}{2}$–11 : 1 years.
This is a sentence completion test assessing word recognition and comprehension and takes about 15 minutes.

d   Young's *Group Reading Test* (ULP), RA 6 : 0–10 : 1 years.
This consists of word recognition and comprehension together

135

with sentence completion, and takes about 20 minutes.

   e Brimer's *Wide Span Reading Test* (Nelson), RA 7–15 years. This consists of sentence completion tests and tests comprehension.

   A very useful book is *The Teacher's Guide to Tests and Testing* by S. Jackson (Longman).

Some basic reading difficulties and suggested methods of treatment

Teachers should regard diagnosis as an essential part of teaching reading and this diagnosis should be continuous because the growth of reading ability depends upon the sequential development of reading skills. The diagnosis of reading ability is more than an assessment of reading because, frequently, the reading difficulties exhibited by a child may reflect many causes of failure. The teacher should plan the reading lessons bearing in mind a child's limitation in reading. Standardised tests and teacher-made tests can be used to ascertain at what level a child can benefit from the teaching.

Poor language development
Certain severe handicaps may well continue into a child's school life. These handicaps may include defective articulation, primitive sentence construction, immature syntax, extensive word-finding difficulties. The teacher must regard the first essential as helping the child to use words as the preferred form of communication. Learning to express feelings and experiences verbally precedes the teaching of more formal features of communication.

Listening
Bramwyche (1972) suggests that the most important factors which make for efficient listening are motivation of the children and the intrinsic interest of the material offered to them. Bramwyche found that many children perform badly in everyday listening tasks, but this may reflect as much on the nature of the tasks set as on the poor performance of the children. It appears that although over 50 per cent of classroom time is spent in listening, proficiency in the listening skills remains low.

136

There are children who experience difficulty in recognising contextual clues in speech; many do not interpret correctly common features of intonation and they exhibit poor ability at detecting the relationship between main and subordinate ideas in an oral statement.

Bramwyche states that one reason given for this is that sheer weight of words causes some children to 'switch off'. Frequently, teachers are unaware of the limited attention span of even the brightest pupils. Another reason given is that listening skills do not function at their best when children have to simply listen to the teacher rather than being able to involve themselves in dialogue. A third reason given is that children are seldom taught to listen.

Considering that we spend 50 per cent of our language skills in listening, it becomes quite apparent that listening plays a very important part in the development of a child's language. Listening ability is very closely related to the reading process and children differ quite appreciably in listening ability. This ability is frequently taken for granted and many children give the impression that they are listening when they are not. Naturally, many activities take place in school which depend on listening, but, frequently, a teacher must be prepared to provide more exercises and activities that are specifically related to listening. Here are a few suggestions:

1 Read out a few sentences describing an object and arrange these sentences in such a way that the children must follow the description very carefully in order to discover what is being described. For example:

> I am made of wood
> You see me in the house
> You walk up me
> Then go to bed   (stairs)

2 Instructions. Give the child a few sentences which must be fully understood in order that a particular instruction may be carried out correctly.

3 Allow groups of children to play games so that each child in turn gives directions to the others.

4 Tell a short story and then ask certain children to tell the story again.

5 Describe a large picture and deliberately use a word which is completely irrelevant.

6 Read the beginning of a short story and then ask certain

137

children to complete it so that the ending fits in logically with the main theme of the story.

7 Allow children to use the tape recorder for various purposes including their own recordings of their stories.

8 Ask certain children to listen to messages and then ask them to deliver them to other children in the class or members of staff.

The SRA Listening Laboratory Project
Listening Laboratory 1b is built round a series of eight cassettes. Each tape contains four listening passages and is devised to develop a particular group of skills. The tapes are at progressive levels of difficulty. The questions following each listening passage exercise the pupil in the particular group of skills concerned and there is a build-up of skills development on a cumulative basis from level to level.

The kit contains 40 workbooks (My Look and Listen Book). A Book Finder Chart suggests further reading for the child on topics that interest him. There is a Teacher's Reference Manual.

Speech defects
Speech defects and various difficulties in articulation due to immature speech development may have adverse effects on learning to read. Certain children become embarrassed during oral reading activities because of their speech difficulties and mispronunciations. These children may withdraw from these activities and emotional distress may well be built up. The situation could become even worse if classmates make fun of these children.

It is not expected that the teacher should diagnose all the difficulties associated with speech defects but there are some which the teacher should be able to recognise, and distinguish from those that are less serious. It is necessary for a speech specialist to deal with cases of stuttering, cleft-palate speech, whispered or almost voiceless speech, mutism and speech affected by hearing defects.

Certain common speech difficulties may be recognised and treated by the teacher. Lisping involves the mispronunciation of the s, z, sh and ch sounds. Infant children may exhibit lisping in several ways:

th is substituted for s
l is substituted for s

138

sh is substituted for s

s may be pronounced with air passing through the nose instead of the mouth.

Difficulties in articulation may include substitutions of sounds, omissions or transpositions. Difficulties may arise with the articulation of many consonants including the following sounds:

j, l, r, v, g, s, z, sh, ch, th (thin), th (that) and wh.

In some cases these difficulties may result from malformation of the mouth, incorrect fitting of the jaws or incomplete teeth formation. The following are examples of the most frequent substitutions experienced by young children:

f, v, for th (thin), th (that), e.g. fing for thing; vere for there.

t, d for th (thin), th (that), e.g. tin for thin; dat for that.

s for th (thin), e.g. sink for think.

b for v, e.g. bery for very.

t, d for k, g, e.g. tat for cat; date for gate.

Poor visual perception and discrimination

A child must be able to make fine discriminations in order to read effectively. The teacher can help the child sharpen his powers of visual perception and discrimination through experience and practice. It is important that she remembers that, when she is devising material to assist the child's powers of visual perception and discrimination, learning should be based on small steps to begin with, easier exercises before complex ones, ensuring that the child knows the results of his efforts, and praise is given together with frequent encouragement and revision.

If a child is experiencing difficulty in learning to recognise the difference between letter shapes then one should assist him by providing him with material which involves the sense of feel and movement as well as sight. Allow the child to trace the difficult letters. Encourage him to write the letter in the air and on the blackboard. Provide him with a letter made of sandpaper. Encourage him to make the letter out of materials such as plasticine and pipe cleaners. Supply the child with letter-dominoes for matching exercises. A useful game is Letter Bingo, one child shows a letter and the other child, with a letter-card, covers this letter with a counter. Show the child pairs of pictures. Some pairs should be identical whereas others should have slight differences. Ask the child to say whether the pictures are the same or different. Ask him to pick the odd man out from six pictures. This exercise may be varied so that the odd man out may be slightly different from the rest or it may belong to a different classification. Prepare several silhouettes of well-known objects, etc. and ask the child to select the object which is called out.

A graded series of exercises can be based on activities designed to develop the following skills:

1 The ability to recognise identical geometrical figures.
2 The ability to recognise geometrical figures where finer discriminations are required.
3 The ability to recognise objects containing small differences.
4 The ability to recognise identical numbers.
5 The ability to recognise letters.
6 The ability to recognise small words.
7 The ability to find certain letters in a word.
8 The ability to find a certain letter in a sentence.
9 The ability to recognise identical beginnings in words.
10 The ability to recognise identical endings in words.
11 The ability to recognise word families.
12 The ability to appreciate the length of words.
13 The ability to appreciate the difference between words of the same length but with significantly different configurations.
14 The ability to appreciate the difference in the appearance of words beginning with capital and lower case letters.
15 The ability to appreciate the difference between singular and plural forms of words.
16 The ability to appreciate the two smaller words in a compound word.

Here are a few examples for skills 1 to 11:

1

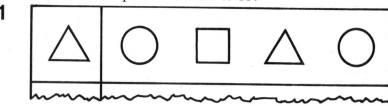

(which of the four on the right is exactly the same as the one on the left? The child is told to underline or colour.)

2

3

4

| 6 | 2 | 5 | 9 | 6 |

5

| u | n | m | u | w |

6

| here | hear hare here head |

7

| e | be pencil kite money |

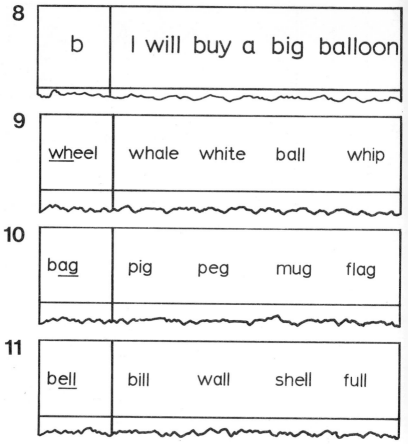

Poor auditory perception and discrimination

A check on hearing may be carried out by using the 'Hearing Test Cards' obtainable from the Royal National Institute for the Deaf, 105 Gower St., London WC1. Each card contains four pictures whose names have the same vowels but different consonants. Stand behind the child and say—'Point to the ......' If the child is to select the correct picture from a set, he must be able to hear the consonants, e.g. house, mouse, owl, cow.

Many children experiencing reading difficulty exhibit poor auditory perception and discrimination. Frequently, these children do not suffer from hearing loss but experience difficulty in discriminating between rather fine differences in sounds. These children often wrongly pronounce or incorrectly accent certain words. There is frequent confusion of similar consonants and vowels, e.g. p–b, v–f, g–k, etc. Many of these children require a certain amount of drill and activities in order to develop their powers of auditory perception and discrimination and it is very important that they receive abundant practice in recognising letters seen and heard. Here are a few suggestions for helping the child develop auditory perception and discrimination:

1 It may be necessary to use everyday sounds with some children. The sounds of animals can be used, such as the sounds of cows, sheep, dogs, cats, ducks and so on.
2 Discriminate rhyming words:
   a   gun, fun, fire, run
   b   bell, shell, well, ball
   c   boat, bat, coat, goat
   d   sheep, shoe, sleep, keep
   e   night, light, horse, fight.
3 Riddles:
You drink it and it begins with 'mi'.
You sleep in it and it begins with 'be'.
4 Initial letter sounds: The teacher says a few words beginning with a particular letter, e.g. bag, balloon, Ben, ball. She emphasises the initial sound 'b' and asks the child to think of other words beginning with the same sound.
5 Concentrate on a particular sound. Use riddles as follows:
   a   I have one. It barks. (dog)
   b   It's a name. A boy's name.
        It rhymes with 'can'. (Dan)
   c   Six times two—that is twelve or? (dozen)
6 Different word beginnings and word endings:
The teacher says three or four or five words all beginning with or ending with the same sound except for one. The child is asked to pick the 'odd-man-out', e.g.
     can, fan, car, man
     peg, pool, big, pig
7 Start a story, e.g. The man went shooting. He took a g—.
8 Whose voice? Children close their eyes and one child recites a poem.
9 It may be necessary in certain cases to help the child with his tongue and lip movements when he is trying to make certain sounds.

Poor directional attack

The majority of children learn the correct sequence of reading from left to right but a few who experience reading difficulty may require additional exercises to help develop left/right orientation. The teacher can provide the child with many activities that will assist him in left to right sequence. A few reading schemes have workbooks that contain exercises in left to right practice. But the teacher will probably have to provide additional materials and exercises:

1 The child can be encouraged to draw a line from left to right over a series of dots.

2 Provide the child with a series of action pictures which have to be followed from left to right. Comics and annuals contain such action pictures. Other examples may be found in non-verbal intelligence tests.

3 Provide the child with pictures that help to encourage left to right movements, e.g. a picture of a boy throwing a ball from left to right with his dog running from left to right to collect it.

4 Give the child separate action pictures so that he has to arrange them in a correct order from left to right in order to understand the sequence of the story.

5 Mazes. The child has to move his finger or pencil from left to right in order to find his way out of the maze. Other mazes may involve animals, e.g. a mouse on the left-hand side and a piece of cheese on the right.

6 Give the child a few well-known words and ask him to put them in the correct order and read the sentence, e.g.:

SEE   THE   I   DOG   BLACK

Reversals

Some children suffering from reading disability may tend to reverse letters, words or phrases. The reversing of such letters as 'b' and 'd' and 'p' and 'q' is common amongst some children. It is useful to show a child that he can change the lower case 'b' into a capital B by adding a loop at the top which goes in the same direction as the bottom loop. Provide the child with rows of letters and ask him to underline all the 'b's.

Print the word 'bed' on the blackboard or on a piece of paper. Tell the child that when the word is printed he must remember that there must be bedposts at each end. In the word 'bed', emphasise that the first letter has the sound 'b' and the last

144

the sound 'd'.

Emphasise the direction of reading by using exercises involving finger contact, underlining or the use of a sand tray. It is interesting to note that children rarely reverse the 'b' and 'd' in cursive writing. A cursive 'b' can be traced over a printed 'b' and the same can be done with the letter 'd'. The children may be told that the cursive letters go in the same direction as the printed ones.

If a child continues to reverse the letter 'q', he can be told that 'q' is always followed by 'u'. Some children continue to reverse such words as 'was' for 'saw', 'no' for 'on' 'pat' for 'tap' and so on. The teacher should encourage the child to sound out the first letter of each word. The teacher could pronounce the words correctly and then ask the child to repeat them. Exercises may be devised for those children who continue to reverse words in their reading. Provide the child with sentences with alternatives but which will only make sense if the correct words are selected. For example,

1 Put your hat $\frac{\text{no}}{\text{on}}$ your head

2 We $\frac{\text{saw}}{\text{was}}$ a tiger at the zoo

3 I caught a fish in my $\frac{\text{net}}{\text{ten}}$

4 My $\frac{\text{dog}}{\text{god}}$ will bite you

5 Water comes from the $\frac{\text{tap}}{\text{pat}}$

Correct eye movements should receive particular attention at this stage and faulty habits should be corrected as early as possible. The teacher should give the child practice in developing a sense of direction from left to right, up and down and so on because some children confuse 'u' and 'n', 'b' and 'p' and 'm' and 'w'. The teacher may draw a large arrow at the top of the page to remind the child to read from left to right.

Establish the kinaesthetic patterns for the letters causing difficulty either by encouraging the child to trace over the words 'dog' and 'bed', at the same time giving the sounds in the words— emphasising the initial sounds, or by guiding the child's forefinger through the patterns of the words in a sand tray—giving the sounds in each word. Other letter confusions such as 'h' and 'k' and 'u' and 'n' can be eradicated by using the above procedure.

Substitutions

Certain children who experience reading difficulty may substitute real words in place of the word in the narrative. Many of these children make substitutions based on the meaning that they are getting from the content of the text or the pictorial clue. Generally speaking, good readers quickly pass this stage but slow readers may experience difficulty at this stage for some time. If the teacher finds that there is frequent substitution, she should use easier material and attempt to enlarge the child's sight vocabulary by using games and activities of various kinds.

On occasions, a child may hesitate when confronted with words which the teacher may regard as fairly common sight words and which, she believes, should be contained in the child's basic vocabulary. The teacher may find that in certain cases the initial letter is the reason for the confusion.

It is wise, therefore, in this case, to encourage the child to attempt the first sound of the word rather than to prompt him in the usual way. The teacher should provide the child with various games in which phonic analysis is emphasised.

Starting errors

When children make errors at the start of words, provide them with several words that have identical endings but with different beginnings. Make lists of words as below. Give one list to the child and retain a copy. Read out the words and ask the child to give you the number of the word which is read out.

1	singing	1	crossed	1	little
2	shopping	2	jumped	2	bottle
3	crossing	3	walked	3	kettle
4	jumping	4	smashed	4	battle
5	running	5	killed	5	rattle
6	walking	6	loved	6	nettle

Ending errors

Use an approach similar to the one above. Use words in which the first three or four letters are identical but with different endings.

1	bark	1	carpet	1	limb
2	bargain	2	carry	2	limit
3	barking	3	cart	3	limping
4	barber	4	carve	4	limped
5	barked	5	carol	5	limited
6	barrel	6	caravan	6	limits

Middle errors

Use an approach similar to the preceding one. Ask the child to call out the number of the word which has been read. Select words that have the same beginnings and ends but with different middles.

1	boat	1	pint	1	mast
2	beat	2	pest	2	must
3	best	3	pant	3	meet
4	beet	4	port	4	most
5	but	5	part	5	meant
6	bat	6	post	6	mint

Ask the child to select the correct words to make sense out of the following sentences:

1 I $\frac{\text{must}}{\text{mast}}$ go to the toilet

2 This ship was in the $\frac{\text{port}}{\text{part}}$

3 I fell and hurt my $\frac{\text{bank}}{\text{back}}$

4 A $\frac{\text{pant}}{\text{pint}}$ of milk, please

5 My mother cooked the $\frac{\text{meat}}{\text{most}}$

6 I can see a sailing $\frac{\text{boat}}{\text{beat}}$

Additions and omissions

If the children continue to add or omit words, the teacher should use cards containing incomplete sentences and completed ones. Here, the child compares one card with the other. Furthermore, the teacher should also ensure that more emphasis is placed on the meaning of the words being read. One very important way to help the child overcome additions and omissions is to allow him to read with you. If certain children continue to omit lines, then the teacher should provide them with reading material which has wide line spacing. The teacher may also allow the children to underline each line of print while it is being read. Because of continued difficulty, a teacher may have to provide a 'reading mask' which reveals one line at a time (see over).

```
┌ ─ ─ ─ ─ ─ ─ ─ ─ ─ ─ ─ ─ ┐
│   They went into the park   │
└ ─ ─ ─ ─ ─ ─ ─ ─ ─ ─ ─ ─ ┘

    ┌─────────────────────────┐
    │   They saw many flowers  │
    └─────────────────────────┘
```

A child's reading ability should be evaluated before teaching begins. A teacher of first year juniors should study the record kept by the previous teacher and then diagnosis should be continuous, based on a daily and weekly basis. There is a danger that the initial teaching may be too difficult for the child and he may have to be put on a lower level. The teacher should devise her own reading tests based on the books being read by the child.

Transpositions
Certain children may transpose one or two letters within a word. For example, a child may read 'form' for 'from'. Transpositions usually result from a child's concentration on the end of the word. Select those words being transposed and include these in sentences. Ask the child to select the correct word and so make sense out of the sentence.

1   I left / felt the house and went to school

2   We put the baby in the parm / pram

3   I am eating a bag of crisps / crips

4   We keep two rabbits as pets / pests

5   The bird flew into its nest / nets

6   The man works on a fram / farm

A general approach to the problem of reading failures

A Report of the Advisory Committee on Handicapped Children (Children with Specific Reading Difficulties, 1972) suggests an approach to the problem of children suffering from reading backwardness:

1 In collaboration with educational psychologists and school medical officers, teachers should screen all children for reading backwardness, preferably at the end of the infant stage.

2 Both the schools and educational psychologists should maintain a continuing check for as long as necessary on the subsequent progress of children identified as backward in reading.

3 Children who are backward in reading, including those with specific reading backwardness, should normally be given skilled remedial teaching in their ordinary schools.

4 Particular attention should be given to the needs of children with reading backwardness in secondary schools, each of which (apart from grammar schools) should have at least one teacher skilled in the remedial teaching of reading.

5 All schools should give careful consideration to the best means of utilising skills and experience of their specialists in the remedial teaching of reading, both directly in the teaching situation and as a source of advice to other members of staff.

6 Where they do not already exist, Remedial Education Centres should be set up for the small number of children who need to be withdrawn for their ordinary schools for either part-time or short full-time remedial sessions.

7 Remedial Education Centres should work in close

collaboration with ordinary schools, and in this, as in other ways, should contribute to the wider dissemination of good remedial teaching techniques relating to reading backwardness.

8 For children with prolonged specific reading backwardness, full use should be made of oral learning methods, and there should be, where necessary, arrangements for oral assessment in internal, and, if possible, also in external examinations.

9 Authorities should review their provision for those who leave school without adequate reading skills. Such provision should include arrangements for a fuller investigation of those who present unusual problems.

An assessment sheet used for readiness for the beginning stages of reading

The following assessment sheet is intended as a guide for teachers who wish to develop their own assessment sheet to judge a child's readiness for the tasks in the beginning stages of learning to read.

Readiness for the beginning stages of reading

Surname ....

Christian names ....

Date of birth..

1 Mental Level

Above Average/Average/Below Average
i Based on class observations: ....
ii IQ (if known)...
iii Mental age (if known)...

2 Physical and Perceptual factors

i Vision
Normal/Below Normal
a Have eyes been tested?...........Results ....
b Are there signs of visual discomfort? ....
c Visual discrimination:
Can the child match printed letters? ....
printed words?...........printed sentences? ....
Can he detect minor differences in certain words, e.g.
bit, bite; dig, big; hot, hut? ....

ii Hearing
Normal/Below Normal
a Has hearing been tested?...........Results..................
b Are there signs of hearing difficulties? ....
c Auditory discrimination:
Does he appreciate the same initial sounds in such words
as but, butter, butterfly, bun, bus?............................
Does he appreciate rhyme in such words as bell, well,
shell, sell? ....
Does he appreciate the same middle sounds in such
words as cat, bat, fat, hat, mat? ....

iii Speech
a Does the child lisp or stutter?.................................
b Is he receiving treatment? ....

iv Physical condition
Normal/Below Normal
Other comments ....
....

3 Home Environment

    a Are there books in the home?....................................

    b Does someone read to him at home?.........................

    c Do the parents help in reading?..............................

    d Is English spoken at home?....................................

4 Emotional Factors

    a Are there serious emotional problems?.........................

    b Has the child put up a barrier against reading?.............

    c Does he appreciate the enjoyment that may be obtained from books?...

    d What are the child's special interests?.........................

5 Language Development

    a Can he repeat nursery rhymes or poems?.....................

    b Can he tell a short story from memory?.....................

    c Does he attend during story telling?...........................

    d Does he show enjoyment when listening to stories?..........

    e Does he appreciate the difference between a printed word and a picture?..

    f Does he appreciate the meaning of such terms as 'number', 'letter' and 'word'?..

    g Can he talk about an illustration using sentences with four or more words?..

    h Is he able to describe his own personal experiences?.........

    i Is he able to say the missing word in a rhyme he knows? ....

    j Is he able to classify? For example: All these are toys. All these are animals. All these we wear. All these things we eat...

    k Does he enjoy looking at picture books?.....................

    l Does he handle books with care?..............................

    m Can he write or print his own name?.........................

    n Does he ask what certain symbols say?.........................

Other comments...
....
....

Assessment of phonic skills

Name.. Sex ....

Date of birth...........................

Age....................years ....months

Assessment summary

Sections

	1	2	3	4	5	6	7	Total
	initial vowel sounds	initial consonant sounds	short middle vowel sounds	long vowel sounds	initial consonant blends and digraphs	final consonant blends and digraphs	vowel digraphs and diphthongs	
max. score	5	20	5	4	26	12	18	90
actual								

Assessment details

(Place a cross (X) under each error)

Section 1

a^1	e^2	i^3	o^4	u^5

Section 2

b^6	c^7	t^8	p^9	j^{10}	r^{11}	n^{12}	d^{13}	l^{14}	m^{15}	s^{16}	g^{17}	k^{18}	f^{19}

v^{20}	w^{21}	h^{22}	y^{23}	z^{24}	q^{25}

Section 3

a^{26}	e^{27}	i^{28}	o^{29}	u^{30}

Section 4

a^{31}	i^{32}	o^{33}	u^{34}

Section 5

fl^{35}	fr^{36}	pl^{37}	cl^{38}	cr^{39}	gr^{40}	bl^{41}	tr^{42}	br^{43}	dr^{44}	sk^{45}	sw^{46}	gl^{47}	wh^{48}

sp^{49}	pr^{50}	st^{51}	sm^{52}	sn^{53}	sl^{54}	ch^{55}	sh^{56}	th^{57}	qu^{58}	th^{59}	sc^{60}

Section 6

sk^{61}	nk^{62}	ft^{63}	st^{64}	sp^{65}	nt^{66}	ch^{67}	sh^{68}	ct^{69}	ld^{70}	th^{71}	nd^{72}

oa^{73}	ea^{74}	ee^{75}	oo^{76}	ai^{77}	oi^{78}	au^{79}	ou^{80}	ie^{81}	aw^{82}	ow^{83}	ew^{84}	oy^{85}

Section 7

ay^{86}	ue^{87}	ow^{88}	oo^{89}	ea^{90}

Assessment of phonic skills: Teacher's notes

This test is basically a diagnostic instrument. The aim is to provide the teacher with information concerning a child's strengths and weaknesses in various areas of phonic knowledge. The test consists of 7 sections as follows:

1 Initial vowel sounds: a, e, i, o, u
2 Initial consonant sounds: b, c, t, p, j, r, n, d, l, m, s, g, k, f, v, w, h, y, z, q
3 Short middle vowel sounds: a, e, i, o, u
4 Long vowel sounds: a, i, o, u
5 Initial consonant blends and digraphs: fl, fr, pl, cl, cr, gr, bl, tr, br, dr, sk, sw, gl, wh, sp, pr, st, sm, sn, sl, ch, sh, th, qu, th, sc
6 Final consonant blends and digraphs: sk, nk, ft, st, sp, nt, ch, sh, ct, ld, th, nd
7 Vowel digraphs and diphthongs: oa, ea, ee, oo, ai, oi, au, ou, ie, aw, ow, ew, oy, ay, ue, ow, oo, ea

The test consists of 90 sets. Each set tests one phonic element which is placed in a set of four other phonic elements.

The test may be used with groups of children or with individuals. The teacher should ask the child to look at Set 1:

"Put a ring around the letters that say 'ab'."

Use the same procedure with all sets. But the teacher must continually ensure that the children are studying the correct set before calling out the phonic element.

Phonic elements should be called out in the following order:

Section 1:	1	ab	2	ep	3	im	4	od	5 ug
Section 2:	6	bab	7	cam	8	tid	9	pep	10 jan
	11	rup	12	nog	13	dat	14	lig	15 mut
	16	sem	17	gud	18	kib	19	fap	20 vag
	21	wid	22	hep	23	yen	24	zut	25 quan
Section 3:	26	bap	27	ted	28	gip	29	gog	30 hun
Section 4:	31	gabe	32	tipe	33	bote	34	tute	
Section 5:	35	flig	36	fran	37	plad	38	clog	39 crin
	40	gren	41	blup	42	tron	43	brud	44 drog
	45	skat	46	swit	47	glig	48	whad	49 spen
	50	prat	51	stup	52	smen	53	snat	54 slet
	55	chig	56	shox	57	thun	58	quax	59 thet
			60	scen (sk)					
Section 6:	61	dask	62	senk	63	luft	64	lest	65 wusp
	66	pent	67	tarch	68	bish	69	fect	70 feld
	71	beth	72	bund					
Section 7:	73	doat	74	gean	75	jeet	76	gook	77 kail
	78	roin	79	taul	80	foud	81	nied	82 tawn
	83	gowl	84	bew	85	loy	86	vay	87 gue
	88	fown	89	hoon	90	nead (short sound)			

It is advisable to test the children on the first 34 sets and then allow them to take a rest before moving on to the remainder of the test. (A second rest period may be required at the end of Set 60.)

At the end of the test the cover page should be completed and so provide a detailed guide to the child's strengths and weaknesses in various areas of phonic knowledge. The actual scores for each section should be entered together with the total score out of 90. In the 'Assessment details' section, a cross (X) should be placed under each error. The phonic elements are numbered and correspond to the set-numbers.

Remedial exercises

This test should be used in conjunction with the booklet—*Reading with Phonics* (Evans Brothers). This booklet contains remedial exercises for specific phonic weaknesses as follows:

Section in test	Relevant page in *Reading with Phonics*		
1 Initial vowel sounds	19	—	20
2 Initial consonant sounds	11	—	18
3 Short middle vowel sounds	19	—	20
4 Long vowel sounds	19	—	20
5 Initial consonant blends and digraphs	23	—	25
6 Final consonant blends and digraphs	23	—	25
7 Vowel digraphs and diphthongs	26	—	27

More detailed suggestions for remedial exercises may be obtained from *Phonics and the Teaching of Reading* (Evans Brothers).

Section One:

Initial vowel sounds:	1	eb	2	ap	3	am	4	ad	5	og
		ab		ip		im		id		ug
		ib		ep		um		od		eg
		ob		op		em		ud		ig
		ub		up		om		ed		ag

TOTAL:

Section Two:

Initial consonant sounds:	6	rab	7	bam	8	wid	9	dep	10	han
		bab		fam		fid		hep		jan
		gab		cam		tid		pep		pan
		lab		ram		gid		tep		ban
		tab		tam		bid		fep		san
	11	gup	12	cog	13	gat	14	gig	15	dut
		pup		mog		jat		hig		fut
		sup		gog		lat		lig		mut
		rup		tog		dat		nig		jut
		bup		nog		tat		rig		lut
	16	bem	17	fud	18	gib	19	hap	20	mag
		lem		gud		hib		bap		vag
		mem		rud		kib		jap		pag
		pem		sud		pib		fap		cag
		sem		hud		wib		wap		hag
	21	fid	22	bep	23	gen	24	fut	25	san
		pid		lep		jen		mut		jan
		tid		mep		yen		tut		quan
		gid		dep		nen		zut		gan
		wid		hep		wen		wut		lan

TOTAL:

Section Three:

Short middle vowel sounds:	26	bep	27	tad	28	gep	29	geg	30	han
		bap		ted		gap		gag		hon
		bip		tid		gup		gig		hin
		bop		tud		gop		gug		hun
		bup		tod		gip		gog		hen

TOTAL:

Section Four:
Long vowel
sounds:

31 gob	32 tip	33 bot	34 tot
gabe	tep	bate	tute
geb	tipe	bute	tut
gube	tape	bote	tat
gib	tup	bet	tete

TOTAL:

Section Five:
Initial consonant
blends and
digraphs:

35 shig	36 cran	37 clad	38 shog	39 smin
flig	dran	prad	slog	crin
chig	span	plad	spog	flin
drig	fran	stad	trog	slin
slig	skan	swad	clog	brin
40 gren	41 shup	42 chon	43 crud	44 prog
blen	crup	tron	flud	drog
sten	blup	bron	slud	blog
shen	slup	dron	brud	stog
bren	stup	ston	plud	crog
45 crat	46 brit	47 blig	48 shad	49 chen
slat	swit	shig	chad	gren
plat	flit	flig	whad	shen
skat	stit	glig	clad	spen
grat	clit	slig	slad	sken
50 drat	51 chup	52 shen	53 flat	54 shet
slat	drup	spen	slat	slet
prat	shup	smen	clat	stet
trat	stup	swen	snat	swet
clat	flup	sten	trat	cret
55 drig	56 flox	57 chun	58 grax	59 flet
flig	shox	grun	scax	thet
chig	blox	thun	spax	spet
shig	slox	spun	quax	bret
slig	snox	skun	shax	chet
60 clen				
flen				
scen				
spen				
sten				

TOTAL:

158

Section Six:
Final consonant blends and digraphs:

61 dant	62 sent	63 lunt	64 lend	65 wuth
dask	selt	luft	lemp	wunk
dang	selk	lund	leng	wusp
dath	senk	lung	lest	wuch
dash	seck	lush	lene	wush
66 penk	67 tath	68 bith	69 fect	70 fenk
peck	tald	bish	fest	feld
peng	tarch	bift	feng	fert
pent	tang	bick	fesh	feg
peng	tass	bisk	fesp	fer
71 besk	72 buck			
beck	buld			
besh	bund			
beth	bunk			
bech	bung			

TOTAL:

Section Seven:
Vowel digraphs and diphthongs:

73 deet	74 goon	75 joot	76 geek	77 keel
doat	gean	jite	gike	kail
deat	goan	jeet	guck	kole
doot	gorn	jort	gook	koil
diet	gine	jarm	gake	koul
78 rane	79 teal	80 fead	81 noad	82 tarn
roon	taul	foud	nend	tawn
roan	teel	foad	nied	town
roin	tail	fard	nard	tean
rant	tull	fand	nord	tine
83 gell	84 baw	85 lay	86 voy	87 goe
gall	bew	loy	vey	gue
gull	bow	luy	vay	gie
gowl	biw	liy	viy	gai
gawl	buw	ley	vuy	gea
88 forn	89 hoan	90 nead		
fown	hean	nood		
furn	hain	need		
feen	hoon	neard		
farn	hine	nind		

TOTAL:

Chapter 10

Reading failures: an investigation

Many claims have been put forward for the efficiency of various reading experiments, remedial methods, etc., and the relative success of such experiments as determined by the gain in reading age by a varying number of pupils. Such investigations include those of Schonell (1948a), Schonell and Wall (1949), Ace (1956), Dunham (1960), Hillman and Snowdon (1960), Roberts (1960), and Shearer (1967). Many investigators, notably Collins (1961) and Lovell *et al.* (1962, 1963), have raised doubts about the long-term effects of remedial education. Curr and Gourlay (1960) have emphasised this point and have stressed the large practice effects when children are repeatedly tested during remedial treatment. Kellmer-Pringle and Gulliford (1953) and Kellmer-Pringle (1963) have emphasised that lasting benefit can be derived from remedial treatment only when it involves creative and therapeutic activities as well as knowledge of the child's background, problems and parental attitudes. Cashdan *et al.* (1971) studied over 1,200 children receiving remedial teaching in reading. They found that IQ was unrelated to any real extent to improvement in reading. It is suggested that the most one can say at the moment is that despite the general correlation between IQ and attainment, some children find learning to read difficult, irrespective of their measured intelligence'. It was also found that lateral dominance and crossed laterality did not matter very much, and it is suggested that orientation difficulties are more important in the poor reader than questions of dominance.

However, with all this excellent work, it is frequently noted that little is mentioned of those children involved in various experiments who still continue to fail in reading. Vernon (1960) showed her concern for this problem when she discussed the claims put forward for various remedial methods and experiments —'valuable supplementary evidence could be obtained, however, by discovering how many failed to profit by them, and continued to show an appreciable degree of backwardness'.

An opportunity existed to carry out an investigation which, it was hoped, would help to fill the gap referred to by Vernon and, maybe, meet the needs of many colleagues in the field of Special Education. Remedial teachers are repeatedly confronted with the problem of having to deal with children who still continue to fail in reading, while the majority, receiving the same special educational treatment, may make progress. It was hoped that a fairly detailed study of 'improvers' and 'non-improvers' would bring to light significant differences between the two groups which would account for the wide discrepancy in reading attainment between the two groups at the end of an intensive period of remedial treatment.

The design of the investigation

The main objective was to investigate factors causing limited improvement in the reading attainment of a group of children after a sustained period of remedial treatment; and to ascertain whether these factors were found to a greater extent in this group than in another balanced group that had shown a highly significant improvement after the same period of remedial treatment.

The investigator carried out remedial teaching of reading at five primary schools. Seventy-eight children received remedial teaching in groups varying in size from three to six pupils. Each school was visited twice weekly. Each group received approximately 72 lessons of 35 minutes duration from September to the following July (i.e. approximately 42 hours of instruction during a period of 10 months).

The research sample consisted of two groups of twenty children selected from the total of seventy-eight children. Each child was paired according to non-verbal test score, chronological age, sex, socio-economic status and reading age at the beginning of the remedial treatment.

The investigation involved:
1 An inquiry into:
   a whether reading attainment was associated with non-verbal test score, social maturity, emotional and personality adjustment, language development (in the vocabulary sense), · socio-economic background,

161

attendance, handedness, cerebral dominance, right-left disorientation and physical defects;

b whether gain in reading age was related to the mental level of the child as measured by a non-verbal test;

c whether significant differences between the two groups, when compared according to the above factors, accounted for the wide discrepancy in reading attainment between the two groups at the end of 10 months' remedial treatment.

2 The testing of the hypotheses that:

a reading attainment was related to the overall rate of development;

b the group showing persistent reading failure exhibited a higher average number of adverse·characteristics.

3 A search for cases of specific reading disability.

Tests and methods of assessment
The many histograms, graphs and statistical data contained in this investigation have been omitted to allow for easy reading of the results. Reference to statistical data has also been reduced to a minimum but the terms 'correlation', 'not significant', 'significant' and 'highly significant' have been used.

The statistical techniques used were:

a The Product-Moment method of calculating correlation coefficients.

b The 't' test to find significant differences between means and mean gains.

The tests and methods of assessment were as follows:

1 Intelligence: NFER Picture Test 1 and NFER Non-Verbal Test 5.

2 Reading attainment: The Burt (Rearranged) Word Reading Test.

3 Spelling: Schonell's *Graded Word Spelling Tests* A and B.

4 Arithmetic: Schonell's *The Essential Mechanical Arithmetic Test.*

5 Drawing age: Goodenough's 'Drawing of a Man' Test.

6 Vocabulary: The Holborn Vocabulary Test for young children.

7 Handedness, cerebral dominance and right/left disorientation: The use of an adaptation of Benton's (1959) tests for right/left discrimination and the investigator's own tests for handedness and cerebral dominance.

8 Physical condition:
a Health of the child: Children were classified according to 'good', 'fair' or 'poor' general health as recorded on the school record cards. The assistance of class teachers was enlisted. An assessment of the general health of the children during pre-school years was obtained from parents.
b Physical build: Weights and heights were obtained for the whole of the research sample plus a random selection of 20 other children for comparison purposes.
c Other defects: Further information was obtained from school records, teachers, parents and school nurses on vision, hearing, nose, throat, speech, asthma, bed-wetting, etc. (See summary in Appendix A.)

9 School conditions: The investigator obtained information on the following aspects of the school environment:
a adequacy of school buildings;
b accommodation of children;
c liaison between infant and junior schools;
d experience and training of teachers;
e transfer and promotion;
f methods and materials used for the teaching of reading.

10 School attendance: Percentage attendance was obtained for the period of the investigation for (a) school and (b) remedial class. Percentage attendance was also obtained for the previous year. The education welfare officer provided further information.

11 Social competence: The Vineland Social Maturity Scale (Doll, 1953). Calculations were based on the investigator's observations and his questioning of the child.

12 Emotional and personality adjustment: A five-point rating scale based on the LEA's Cumulative Record Card. Assessments were based on the investigator's and class teachers' findings. The characteristics assessed were self-confidence, sociability, co-operation, perseverance, conscientiousness and emotional stability.

13 Socio-economic background: A five-point rating scale. Assessments were based on the findings of the investigator,

education welfare officer, school nurses, class teachers, headteachers, etc. This factor was studied under the headings (a) Cultural, (b) Material and Economic, (c) Motivational and (d) Emotional.

a   Cultural

Information in this category was concerned with such factors as the educational level of the parents, the books in the home, the reading habits of the parents and their leisure interests.

b   Material and Economic

Information in this category was concerned with the income of parents and siblings, and general living conditions as measured by the number of rooms in the house in relation to the number of persons sharing them. The investigator wished to ascertain the degree of overcrowding and so he decided to devise a Living Space Index for each research case. It was decided that the ideal living space for this particular locality was a six-roomed house, i.e. three bedrooms (and a bathroom), a living room, a dining-room and a kitchen for a family of two parents and three children. The following formula for a Living Space Index was devised:

$$\text{Living Space Index:} \ \frac{\text{Number of Rooms}}{\text{Number of Persons}}$$

The ideal Living Space Index for five people living in a six-roomed house was:

$$\frac{6}{5} = 1\cdot2$$

Taking 1·2 as the Ideal Living Space Index, the following comments were used for the following indices:

1·1 to 1·0	Fairly comfortable
0·9 to 0·8	Overcrowded
0·7 and below	Very overcrowded

c   Motivational

In this category, the relevant items are those concerned with the parents' attitudes toward the child's educational progress and future employment, and the encouragement the parents give him in his work.

d   Emotional

In this category, the relevant information comprises the

degree of harmony in the home, the emotional security of the child, and the interest taken by the parents in the child's general welfare.

Criteria were established so that each of the following was regarded as an adverse home factor:

i   father unskilled or unemployed;
ii   mother working full-time;
iii no adult books in the home;
iv   overcrowded home—below 0·9 on Living Space Index;
v   very limited parental leisure activities;
vi   misdirected children's leisure activities;
vii very low income;
viii lack of parental interest in child's education and future employment;
ix   any aspect of an adversely emotional home atmosphere;
x   no reading by child at home.

A value of one point was given for each adverse factor. These were then collated and used in the Five-Point Rating Scale.

The schools

The schools used for the investigation were typical of the many very old primary schools throughout the British Isles. They were either full to capacity or overcrowded. The schools were situated on the eastern edge of the South Wales Coalfield and the building programme for new schools was still many years behind. A few schools were fortunate to have demountable classrooms. The number of children in the five schools ranged from 74 to 263 and the total school population was approximately 900. Overcrowding and lack of adequate accommodation were the investigator's biggest headache. The eventual arrangements were frequently far from ideal. Remedial groups were taught in a chapel vestry, a school hut, a staff room, a store room, and a school canteen. Playground facilities were poor and if a headteacher were fortunate enough to have additional accommodation in the form of a demountable classroom then, frequently, a corresponding area of playground was lost.

The relationship between staff and pupils was based on authoritarian principles and, generally, it was firm and kindly.

Children were streamed into classes by the regular application of intelligence and attainment tests. Methods of teaching were generally orthodox. Headteachers and staff gave the investigator abundant assistance and there was continual liaison between the respective class teachers and the investigator.

Selection of children for remedial teaching

Selection for admission to the remedial groups was made after each child had been discussed with the headteacher and class teacher concerned. Initial selection was based on whether a child was two years or more below the average reading attainment appropriate to his age.

A total of eighty-four children were referred as a result of the initial selection procedure. The NFER Picture Test 1 or the NFER Non-Verbal Test 5 and the Burt (Rearranged) Word Reading Test were administered. The final selection for admission was based on the following criterion: a mental-attainment age discrepancy of two years or more. This method of selection has been attacked by many educationists. P. E. Vernon (1960) states: 'The clinic or educational psychologist should clearly not rely on IQ-EQ discrepancy to pick the cases most likely to benefit from remedial treatment.'

However, many teachers do follow the procedure attacked by Vernon, however unscientific it may be. They maintain that it has a practical value. The investigator believes that his selection procedure was an adequate compromise because even Vernon suggests that 'a teacher's subjective judgment is likely to be a good guide', though he does say that this needs to be supplemented by a thorough investigation of the personality, home, schooling, and other relevant circumstances.

The initial and final selection procedures overcame the possibility of admitting children to remedial classes who would be taking the places of those in most need of such treatment. Out of the final selection of seventy-eight children, twenty-two did not register a score on Burt's reading test. Of the seventy-eight chosen for remedial treatment, seven were under the age of seven years at the beginning of treatment. These children attended one infant/junior school.

Forty-nine boys and twenty-nine girls were selected. The fact that of those requiring remedial treatment only 37·2 per cent were girls and 62·8 per cent were boys supports the finding and views of many educationists. Goodenough (in Carmichael, 1954), as a result of a survey on the sex differences in school performance, reached the conclusion that, on average, girls achieve better results than boys in the first six to eight years of schooling. Her views are supported by many investigators including Monroe (1946), Richardson (1956), Pidgeon (1960), Money (1962), France (1964), Lovell *et al.* (1964), Thackray (1965) and Cashdan *et al.* (1971). Lovell *et al.* (1964) found that during selection of children for their investigation into cognitive and other disabilities in backward readers of average intelligence, there was a far higher proportion of backward boys than girls. This result was obtained on data for 1,205 pupils. An hypothesis was put forward that 'there may be some specific disability affecting the male more than the female'. The reason usually given to explain the disparity in performance between boys and girls is the more rapid maturation of girls.

The following table gives the results obtained at the end of the remedial treatment:

Results of remedial treatment (all children)

Table 1

| No. | Period of treatment | Beginning of treatment | | | | | | End of treatment | | |
		CA	IQ	MA	RA	Retardation	RA	Gain in RA	Retardation
78	months 10	y m 8 7·2	90·64	y m 7 6·8	y m 4 7·1	months 35·7	y m 6 1·9	months 18·8	months 26·0

Table 1 shows a mean gain in reading age of 18·8 months over a period of ten months. The number of children not registering on Burt's Reading Test had fallen from twenty-two to seven. Whereas the majority of children had shown marked improvement in reading attainment, there were, however, many who had shown very limited improvement.

167

Selection of the research sample

In preparation for the investigation, a battery of tests was used on all seventy-eight children early in the first term of treatment. At this time it was possible to make a provisional selection of those children showing undoubted difficulty. But it was not until the end of the second term that one was able to use a criterion for selecting Group A (those showing very limited improvement) and, at the same time, match these, child for child, with those already showing marked improvement. It was decided to select the two groups at the end of the second term in order that home visits could be made. Further tests could be given and assessments could be made with the aid of the headteachers, staff, school nurses, the education welfare officer, the psychiatric social worker and others.

This initial selection of the research sample became, without alteration, the final selection at the end of the school year. The criterion used for the selection of Group A was as follows:

If the child's retardation at the end of March (July, for the final selection) remained the same, or was worse than it was in September.

Twenty children were selected, 12 boys and 8 girls. These were paired, child for child, with children (Group B) who had shown a marked improvement (more than one year in July). The children were paired according to non-verbal test score, chronological age, sex, reading age in September, and socio-economic status.

The final term of the school year became an intensive period of work. Thirty-two of the forty homes were visited with the assistance of the education welfare officer. The investigator was able to collect a tremendous amount of information on the research sample with the help of this invaluable friend and other social workers.

Table 2 opposite shows how the two groups were balanced at the beginning of the investigation according to non-verbal test score and reading age. It shows the significant differences between the two groups in reading age, gain in reading age, and retardation at the end of the investigation.

Comparison of group A with group B

Table 2

Group	Period of treat-ment	Average CA	Average IQ	Average MA	Initial RA	Initial retard-ation	Final RA	Gain in RA	Final retard-ation
A(No.20) B(No.20)	months 10 10	y m 8 0·7 7 10·9	85·15· 86·35	y m 6 11·05 6 11·0	y m 4 1·8 4 5·1	months 33·25 29·95	y m 4 6·6 6 5·6	months 4·8 24·5	months 36·6 13·2
	't' Test	0·600	0·264	0·191	1·562	0·954	7·335	9·550	5·783
Level of signifi-cance of differences of means.		N.S.	N.S.	N.S.	N.S.	N.S.	0·1%	0·1%	0·1%

A five-point rating scale was used to obtain an overall view of the research sample and comprehensive ratings on each child. The factors selected to portray development are each rated on this five-point scale in which the lowest (E) represents a state of affairs that interferes with adjustment and C represents an average state of affairs. The aim here is not so much to provide a measurement but a method of appreciating, at a glance, the areas of weakness. The separate group ratings are set out over the page in Table 3.

Percentage of research cases in each rating category

Table 3

(No. A : 20, B : 20)

Factor	Group	Ratings A	B	C	D	E
Intelligence	A	0	0	35	15	50
	B	0	0	45	10	45
Social Maturity	A	0	0	25	15	60
	B	0	0	45	10	45
Physical Condition	A	0	15	40	40	5
	B	5	25	60	10	0
Educational	A	0	0	10	40	50
	B	0	0	30	50	20
Emotional and Personality Adjustment	A	0	5	55	25	15
	B	0	20	50	25	4
Home: Cultural	A	0	5	10	20	65
	B	5	5	15	35	40
Home: Material and Economic	A	5	5	15	35	40
	B	0	5	10	25	60
Home: Motivational	A	0	5	20	20	55
	B	5	5	5	50	35
Home: Emotional	A	0	5	30	30	35
	B	0	5	10	55	30

Table 3 shows that the research sample was below average on the ratings of intelligence, social maturity, school work and all aspects of socio-economic background. They were average on the ratings for physical condition and emotional/personality adjustment. These ratings are used in this context to indicate the main handicaps affecting the research sample.

A discussion of the results of the investigation

A further reference to Table 1 will show that the mean gain in reading age for the seventy-eight children who received remedial treatment was 18·8 months. This was highly significant and compares favourably with the results obtained by several other investigators. See Table 4 below.

Examples of remedial treatment

Table 4

Investigator	No. of pupils	Average CA		Average MA or IQ		Period of treatment	Initial RA	Gain in RA
		y	m	y	m	months	years	months
Schonell (1942)	31	9	6	8	7	9·1	7·3	15
Schonell & Wall (1949)	11	10	1	10	3	9·0	7·5	12
Ace (1956)								
(a)	33	8	0	7	9	6·0	5·2	19·2
(b)	32	8	0	7	9	6·0	5·2	25·2
Dunham (1960)	20	9	5	IQ 99		6·0	5·7	11
Collins (1961)	20	9	7·5	IQ 96		6·0	6·6	15·2

Intelligence
The findings confirmed previous research that poor intelligence may result in the child having difficulty 'in reasoning out the systematic relationship between word shapes and sounds' (Vernon, 1957). But it was found that the relationship between

171

reading attainment and the level of intelligence was by no means absolute. It was found that several children in the research sample scored fairly highly on the non-verbal test, but their reading was far below that of others who had low non-verbal test scores. Vernon (1957) has suggested that intelligence tests as a rule cover only certain types of reasoning and it may be that these tests are not closely linked to the 'complex reasoning processes which must be employed in learning to read'. Millard (1958) maintains that an intelligence test should respond to maturation and reflect the growth of the whole organism.

It has been suggested that the possibility of failure at the elementary stages of learning to read would be practically eliminated and the effectiveness of teaching would be increased proportionately if the teaching of reading is postponed until the child has reached a certain mental age. Several investigators have been inclined to suggest an absolute relationship between mental age and readiness to read because they have suggested a specific mental age at which a child should be ready to begin reading. But it was found in the present investigation that the relationship between mental age and reading readiness is by no means absolute. At the end of the remedial treatment, seven children from Group B, with a mental age of $6\frac{1}{2}$ or less, had improved on average by 15 months, but seven children from Group A with a mental age of $7\frac{1}{2}$ or more had only improved on average by 5·4 months. Lovell (1963) states: 'Though mental age is without doubt the most important factor in determining the child's readiness for reading, it is not the only one. Previous relevant experience, motivation, the quality of teaching, and the pupil-teacher relationship are also important.'

The investigator concludes that his hypothesis that poor prognosis was due to low intelligence was unfounded. There was a moderately significant correlation[1] between reading age and

1 The meaning of the term Correlation Coefficient. If one wishes to know the significance of some result which has been obtained in an experimental investigation, an appropriate statistical technique may be used. The correlation coefficient tells us the degree of agreement between two sets of scores or orders. It will range from +1·0 if there is perfect agreement between the two sets of scores or orders, 0 if there is no agreement to −1·0 if there is complete disagreement. If the coefficient of correlation is greater than 0·8, the agreement between the two sets of marks or orders is said to be high. If the figure is between 0·4 and 0·7 the relationship may be called moderate.

intelligence. Because the high discrepancy in reading attainment between the two groups cannot be related to any significant difference in non-verbal test score, the investigator was inclined to discount the factor of intelligence as a relevant influence. It is appreciated, however, that because the correlation obtained was not highly significant then neither intelligence nor reading attainment could be predicted one from the other with any degree of confidence. The answer must be looked for elsewhere.

The investigator's hypothesis that gain in reading is related to the mental level of the child was also unfounded. The correlation between gains in reading and mental age did not hold sufficient significance.

Social maturity

The Vineland Social Maturity Scale (Doll, 1953) gives a broader view of adjustment than an intelligence test. It is a series of questions sampling those various social accomplishments that a child can be expected to learn as he grows. Doll advocated the use of this test so that the practical use made of intelligence could be estimated by a measurement of social development. This Vineland Social Maturity Scale measures the ability to grow socially.[2]

A significant correlation was found between social age and reading age. There was no significant difference between the two groups at the beginning of the remedial treatment, but a significant difference at the end. There was also a highly significant gain by Group B over A.

An absolute conclusion would appear to be unsound as the research sample was so small, but it is suggested that remedial treatment has not led to an increase in social competence but rather that the increase in Group B's social competence, together with its increase in reading attainment, is an expression of the total growth of these children. This view is supported by the results obtained from a calculation of a Developmental Age

---

2 In recent years even more attention has been given to the calculation of a factor that can be used to indicate how a child has developed when compared with the level one could expect for an average child. In South Africa (Sunday Times Magazine, 1966) doctors have worked out a factor which they call a Development Quotient. This is regarded as a kind of 'baby' IQ and is based on what the American psychologist Gesell has drawn up as norms for phases of a baby's life up to thirty months. A DQ of 100 would indicate average.

for the whole research sample. (This is discussed later.)

It has been concluded that, since there was a fairly highly significant correlation between social age and reading age, a significant difference in means and a fairly highly significant difference in gains between A and B at the end of the remedial treatment, then social competence is probably a factor determining the difference in reading achievement between two groups.

Emotional and personality adjustment

The investigator did not wish this part of the research to be too unwieldy and so he limited the number of traits under study. But, as a result, only the surface of the problem has been 'scratched'. He supports the views of Vernon (1957) and many others who have advocated investigations of 'possible temperamental or neurotic defect in cases of severe reading disability'. Sampson (1966) has shown concern with the rather inconclusiveness and variability of investigations into emotional and personality adjustment and states that 'the question of the amount of reading backwardness attributable to maladjustment requires careful investigation at different ages and at different IQ levels'. Maybe Kellmer-Pringle (1966) has given a lead with her study of 'Social Learning and its Measurement'. Her study of the measurement of social competence has led to the following statement: 'The child who, compared with his mental level, is markedly advanced or retarded in social competence, is likely also to be emotionally disturbed.'

It is possible that an adaptation of the Vineland Social Maturity Scale could become a useful tool in the diagnosis and treatment of delinquent, maladjusted and backward pupils.

The positive correlations found in this investigation between the six characteristics of emotional and personality adjustment and reading attainment show the relation between emotional and personality adjustment and reading ability and agree with the findings of many other investigators. However, two characteristics, i.e. sociability and co-operation, had low correlations and were not significant. There were significant differences between the two groups for perseverance and conscientiousness and it is suggested that, considering that these two characteristics had the highest correlations with reading age, then they probably had a part to play in accounting for the reading attainment discrepancy between the two groups. But more conclusive evidence was hoped for.

Language development

A relationship was found between level of vocabulary and reading skills. Fairly highly significant correlations were found between vocabulary age and reading age (+0·70) and between vocabulary age and gains in reading (+0·50). These findings agree with those of Sampson (1962) who found a correlation of +0·58 between reading accuracy and vocabulary, and +0·70 between reading comprehension and vocabulary.

It is suggested that the findings point to the probability that Group B were better equipped for tackling reading skills than Group A. It is also probable that the acquisition of this aspect of language development is substantially parallel with the progress of Group B in other aspects of all-round growth.

It is suggested that children should develop an adequate level of vocabulary and oral expression before they can be expected to read and understand the printed thoughts and ideas of others. Schonell (1948b) was well aware of this problem when he stated that children should have adequate activities in their stages of learning to read to create 'a functional language background beforehand'.

Speech defects did not apparently have any relationship to reading ability in this investigation.

Handedness, cerebral dominance and right/left disorientation

Results showed that Group A contained more cases of left-handedness, mixed dominance by right-hand and left-eye preference, and right/left disorientation than Groups B and C (a control group). At first glance there appeared to be an association between these three factors and lack of improvement in reading. However, considering that there were very poor readers, 'improved' readers and 'better' readers (control group) who were left-handed, there does not appear to be conclusive evidence of a relationship between left-handedness and reading disability. It is suggested that left-handedness need not in itself be a handicap to reading even though the act of writing may be affected and the visual feed-back from writing is obscured. It also appears doubtful whether sightedness is of great importance.

Certain investigators have stated that incomplete lateralisation may be an important factor when it is congenital, but one wonders whether this is sufficient to result in permanent reading failure. The research sample included many children who were completely lateralised but who showed reading failure.

175

Conclusive evidence was not found to support a relationship between right/left disorientation and reading failure in the sample.

Socio-economic background

Low positive correlations were found between reading age and the four aspects of socio-economic background (i.e. cultural, material and economic, motivational, and emotional), but only the material and economic aspect had a significant correlation. No significant differences were found between Groups A and B when compared under the four headings. Cultural, material and economic, and motivational conditions varied from poor to very poor in 80 per cent of cases with only 7·5 per cent with good to very good conditions. Ratings for emotional factors were poor to very poor in 80 per cent of cases with only 5 per cent with good conditions. It is suggested that the children had experienced stress because of the physical and mental health of the parents, friction between parents and overcrowding. The average number of persons per home was 7·7 and the average Living Space Index was 0·901. 77·5 per cent of the research sample lived in overcrowded or very overcrowded homes— below 0·9 on the Living Space Index. It must be stated at this juncture that 77·5 per cent of the research cases lived on a new Council Estate catering for slum clearance areas. It is felt that interplay of home conditions and failure in school necessitates a separate investigation.

It is suggested that the detrimental influences of all aspects of the socio-economic background have adversely affected the reading attainment of most of the research cases. Curry (1962) suggests that when a child has above average intellectual ability then he will probably overcome the effects of a deprived home environment, but as the intellectual ability decreases, so the effects of deprived socio-economic conditions will have a more serious effect on his achievements in school. Vernon (1957) has also suggested that the more advanced stages of interest and facility in reading will suffer from a lack of cultural influence found in the poorer homes. Recent work by Davie et al. (1972) confirms these views.

Absenteeism

The results showed a relationship between school attendance and reading attainment with low but positive correlations between reading age and (i) attendance at school ($+0.30$) and (ii) attendance at the remedial class ($+0.27$). There was a fairly highly significant difference between the attendance of the two groups and this indicated that the poor attendance of Group A probably had a detrimental effect on the reading attainment of this group.

It is suggested that failure to read may produce non-attendance almost as much as non-attendance produces reading failure. Throughout the investigation, the investigator frequently noticed that several poor attenders improved in attendance, sometimes remarkably, when they had overcome certain aspects of difficulty in reading. It was found that, in many cases, improvement in attendance ran parallel with improvement in reading. This was particularly noticed with certain members of Group B.

No cases of school phobia were found. These cases have been defined by Kahn (1958), Hersov (1960), Chazan (1962) and Cooper (1966a), i.e. 'those showing neurotic refusal to attend school' (Hersov, 1960). According to Cooper (1966b), school phobics come from homes of a higher social level and they frequently have dominant mothers in over-anxious homes. This description of home environment could not be applied to the vast majority of homes under study in this investigation. The poor and very poor attenders in this investigation were truants and exhibited a pattern allied to their social level. The majority of these truants fitted into the description given by Hersov (1960): 'Children known as truants come from large, ill-disciplined families with little regard for social obligation.'

The most common cause of absenteeism was the deliberate withholding of the child from school by the parents and this was accompanied by apathy on the part of both parents and child. In several cases, the mother of a large family was inclined to keep her child home to assist her with the family. In such cases, the mother was apathetic to the school and the education of her child. The investigator suggests that this apathy is liable to 'rub off' on to the child until he probably becomes more apathetic than the mother. Once the precedent is set, the child takes advantage of the attitude of the parents and, when he is not required at home, he continues to take time off from school to 'enjoy' his own interests.

School conditions

It has already been stressed that the buildings of the five schools were very old and that the main problem was one of overcrowding and inadequate classroom facilities. In three schools, children and staff experienced the inconvenience of using classrooms with curtained partitions. In school A, four classrooms were situated in two large rooms partitioned off with curtains. In this school a chapel vestry was also used as a classroom. In School B, two classrooms were separated by a curtained partition and a school canteen was used as another classroom. Recently, a demountable classroom has been erected at this school. In School C, an old wooden hut was used as a classroom. In School D, two classrooms were separated by curtains.

Such adverse accommodation prevailing at the time of the investigation must surely have had some detrimental effect on the children. Morris (1959) suggests that 'good buildings are associated with a high level of attainment', and Collins (1961) suggests that the 'most obvious cause' of retardation is 'bad teaching environments'. However, children learn in spite of these adverse conditions. There are probably other school conditions with a more detrimental influence on children's progress than school buildings alone.

Generally speaking, the atmosphere, teaching methods and organisation of the five schools were similar. The methods of approach were generally orthodox but one could not say that the approach was too formal. There were opportunities for individual expression in art, drama, games, etc.

The majority of teachers were interested in the problem of children experiencing difficulty in learning to read and this concern was frequently shown.

There was a definite continuity of method where the schools were infant/junior (Schools C, D and E). Two separate infant schools supplied schools A and B. There appeared to be adequate co-operation between schools A and B and one of the infant schools but in the case of the other infant school, more co-operation could have been engendered.

The most commonly used reading scheme was the *Ladybird Key Words Scheme* (Wills and Hepworth). Use was also made of the following schemes, either as main reading schemes or supplementary ones: *The Happy Venture Readers* (Oliver and Boyd); *The Wide Range Readers* (Oliver and Boyd); *The Royal Road Readers* (Chatto and Windus); *Adventures in Reading* (Oxford University Press); *Tom's Day Series* (Collins); and several others.

Generally speaking, in the first-year junior classes, one noticed daily reading practice involving word-building, use of reading apparatus, the making of 'News' books and oral/written work with the use of pictures. The approach to the teaching of reading was a mixture of 'look and say', sentence and phonic work with the phonic work usually following at a later stage.

There were three teachers without experience or training in the teaching of beginning reading and even though they exhibited tremendous enthusiasm, they appeared to be rather lost when confronted with the problem of tackling reading difficulties. Morris (1959, 1966) has emphasised that first-year junior teachers should be familiar with teaching reading from the beginning. I would suggest that a teacher having to teach beginning reading in the junior school should be familiar with the appropriate approach to the problem. The concern here is not so much the inefficiency of the method being used, because a method is as good as the teacher's faith in it, but rather, as Burt (1953) has put it, 'his failure to adapt his methods to the peculiar needs of the backward child'.

It has been suggested that, in certain cases, the time for transfer from the infant to the junior school is too early. It was found that, in the present investigation, three first-year juniors in Group A were probably not ready for transfer from the infant to the junior school. In these cases, the children came from separate infant schools. However, the retention of certain children in the infant school is probably not the answer. Some infant teachers gave the impression that they had to 'prove their existence' by passing on children to the junior school who had started to read. There is a danger here of forcing the slow and unready child, with possible disastrous consequences. The junior school must expect to receive non-readers and be prepared to start them off on the 'reading road'.

Adverse school conditions such as (a) inadequate school buildings, (b) overcrowding, (c) lack of liaison between infant and junior school, (d) teachers not trained or experienced in teaching beginning reading, (e) untimely promotion, may have had a detrimental effect on the reading progress of several of the research sample. However, these conditions applied to approximately equal numbers in Group A and Group B. There seems little doubt that the various aspects of a school will influence the progress of individual children, but many with reading difficulties begin to read in spite of certain adverse conditions.

179

Physical defects

The available evidence suggested that progress in reading could possibly have been impeded by lowered vitality and lowered physical resistance in several cases, and the condition of 'not feeling well' was probably a significant factor in encouraging potential truant to stay away from school. However, the general health of the research sample was fair to good in 85 per cent of the cases. The general condition of the research sample appeared to be that of fatigue rather than illness. This fatigue was probably related to the adverse home circumstances of the majority of the research cases. Many children suffered from the effects of inadequate sleep and irregular meals.

There was not sufficient evidence to warrant an association between the general health and physical condition of the research sample and reading ability. It is possible that several cases suffered from low vitality which resulted in their being inattentive and lacking in concentration. There was no significant difference between the two groups to warrant any justification for the wide discrepancy in reading attainment.

A further study of the research sample

Social maturity, emotional and personality adjustment, language development, socio-economic background, absenteeism and intelligence were found to have positive correlations with reading attainment. It was also found that the probable reasons for the wide discrepancy in reading attainment at the end of the treatment were the significant differences found between Group A and Group B when compared according to social maturity, perseverance and conscientiousness, language development and absenteeism. The investigator considered whether the wide discrepancy in reading attainment between the two groups was primarily due to the difference between the two groups in all-round rate of growth. It was postulated that this factor in Group A was so much at variance with Group B that slowness in learning to read was just one aspect of an overall slow and erratic development rate.

A study of the reading difficulties experienced by the research sample

At the beginning of the investigation and for the following 10 months, there was an attempt to ascertain the difficulties being experienced by the research sample. It was decided to summarise the reading difficulties under five main headings. These headings form a more simplified approach than that of Neale (1958). A summary of the reading difficulties may be seen in Table 5 below.

A summary of reading difficulties experienced by the research sample before and after remedial treatment

Difficulties:

a   Inability to read because the pupils have been unable to perceive and remember the shapes of printed letters.
b   Inability to analyse word shapes into letter shapes.
c   Inability to associate the correct sounds of letters.
d   Inability to combine letter sounds into the sounds of whole words or inability to do this in the correct order.
e   Inability to read words as entities.

Table 5

	Before treatment				After treatment			
	Group A (20)		Group B (20)		Group A (20)		Group B (20)	
Difficulty	Yes	No	Yes	No	Yes	No	Yes	No
a	10	10	6	14	4	16	0	20
b	10	10	6	14	4	16	0	20
c	17	3	12	8	12	8	4	16
d	20	0	14	6	14	6	6	14
e	20	0	16	4	20	0	7	13

Table 5 shows that Group B were at a better stage of readiness for reading than Group A even though there was no significant difference between their reading ages at the beginning of the remedial treatment. Maybe, as Collins (1961) has suggested, many children in Group B had 'known the work all the time but were unwilling to persevere until familiar with the test situation'. Table 5 shows that Group A was at the same stage of readiness at the end of the treatment as Group B was at the beginning. It is possible that some of the research cases, notably those in Group B, overcame reading difficulties quicker than others because of the 'genetic and other influences that cause children to mature at different rates' (Olson, 1959). Is it possible that learning to read is part of the process of growth and, probably as such, is uneven in so far as no two children grow at the same rate; but for each individual child it is a continuous process?

Table 6 shows that not only did Group B show a highly significant improvement in reading over Group A, but also a far better improvement in all school work.

Teachers' remarks on work and behaviour of the research sample at the end of remedial treatment (in percentages)

Table 6

	Work		Behaviour	
	Group A	Group B	Group A	Group B
	(20)	(20)	(20)	(20)
Improved	50	85	45	60
No change	50	15	40	30
Deterioration	0	0	15	10

Table 6 shows that a higher percentage of Group B improved in behaviour than Group A. This improvement in behaviour in the research sample is probably a reflection of the children's feeling of success and achievement in school work, and is probably complementary to the degree of achievement attained. The method of measuring behaviour was based on the class teachers' general observations of each child.

The calculation of a developmental age

Millard (1958), Olson (1959) and Tanner (1961) have propounded the theory that growth in physical maturity and learning are inseparable 'representing a unity which is present throughout the entire period of development' (Millard, 1958).

It was found that the research cases in Group B were slightly taller and heavier than those in Group A but there was no significant difference between the two groups. Tanner (1961) has suggested that 'the age of learning arithmetic and reading should be related to the level of maturation achieved'. He even suggests that 'school leaving age should be determined by developmental age than by chronological age'.

It was decided to calculate a form of developmental age for the research sample in order to ascertain whether the two groups showed a significant difference between their developmental ages and whether such a difference could possibly account for the wide discrepancy in reading attainment between the two groups.

The developmental ages and quotients were calculated as follows:

$$\text{Developmental Age} = \frac{\text{Mental Age} + \text{Social Age} + \text{Vocabulary Age} + \text{Arithmetic Age} + \text{Drawing Age}}{5}$$

$$\text{De. A} = \frac{\text{MA} + \text{SA} + \text{VA} + \text{AA} + \text{DA}}{5}$$

$$\text{Developmental Quotient} = \frac{\text{Developmental Age} \times 100}{\text{Chronological Age}}$$

$$\text{De. Q} = \frac{\text{De. A} \times 100}{\text{CA}}$$

The average developmental age for Group A at the end of the remedial treatment was 6 years 11·5 months and 7 years 7·5 months for Group B. The correlation between developmental age and reading age was +0·70 and was fairly highly significant.

183

The correlation between developmental age and reading age gains was +0·55 and was also fairly highly significant. There was a highly significant difference between means for Group B over Group A.

The fairly highly significant correlations between developmental age and reading age, and reading age gains, and the highly significant differences between the two groups probably account for the wide discrepancy in reading age between the two groups. It is likely that the exceptionally large improvements in reading age in five cases from Group B have been influenced by an equally large improvement in other developmental areas. Another relevant feature is that the average developmental quotient of Group B was 85 as compared with its IQ of 86, but the average developmental quotient of Group A was 76 as compared with its IQ of 85. Investigations have shown that changes occur in IQ (Vernon, 1960), but whether the increase shown by Group B was connected with the remedial treatment is debatable. Collins (1961) found in his investigation that changes in IQ were not connected with remedial education. It is suggested that the average gain of 4·7 on the part of Group B may possibly be a reflection of the group's all-round development.

It appears that if due regard is to be paid to the principles of child development, then the teacher's main concern should be to provide activities appropriate to the rate of development of each individual child. The rate of development will vary not only for each child but also within the individual child's time scale of growth. The difficulty appears to arise when the potential and the rate of development are so greatly disturbed that special remedial treatment is required. External influences such as inept teaching, emotional and personality maladjustment, adverse socio-economic conditions, and absenteeism may have such a detrimental influence that the class teacher may not be able to cater for the child in her own classroom together with thirty-six others, all with their own varying degrees of development.

The calculation of a Reading Index

Many investigators have suggested that something more than a discrepancy between test scores is needed to identify those children who require special help in reading. Both Monroe (1946) and Betts (1950) tried to allow for growth factors by calculating a reading index. In the present investigation, a form of developmental age has been used as a basis for a calculation of a reading index.

$$\text{Reading Index} = \frac{\text{Reading Age}}{\text{Developmental Age}}$$

$$\text{RI} = \frac{\text{RA}}{\text{De. A}}$$

Key to Reading Indices:

$1\cdot00 +$: Special abilities in reading.

$1\cdot00$: Harmonious relationship with other areas of development

Below $1\cdot00$ to $0\cdot80$: Working towards Developmental Age

Below $0\cdot80$ to $0\cdot65$: Reading difficulties

Below $0\cdot65$: Severe reading difficulties

Table 7 on the next page shows the placings of the research sample according to reading indices.

A study of Table 7 shows that 55 per cent of Group A still have reading difficulties and 45 per cent still have severe reading disabilities. In Group B, however, 25 per cent still show reading difficulties but 70 per cent are now working towards their developmental ages. One case exhibited a special ability in reading (RI = $1\cdot06$). The average reading index for Group A was $0\cdot646$ and $0\cdot845$ for Group B.

Throughout the investigation a search was made for cases of 'specific reading disability'. After a study of professional literature many symptoms were found that are used to determine whether a child is suffering from this specific disability, but these were so numerous that it was impossible to draw a line of demarcation between a 'specific reading disability' and other types of reading difficulties. Such symptoms as reversals, additions, omissions, right-left disorientation, etc. were found in Groups A and B and in Group C (the random sample). Symptoms were found in 'very poor readers' (Group A), 'improved readers' (Group B) and 'better readers' (Group C). The findings agreed with those of Malmquist (1958), Morris (1966) and Collins (1961) who suggest that reading disabilities are not isolated effects, 'for failing pupils deviate from the mean of the normal population in many factors in addition to reading' (Malmquist, 1958).

185

Research sample categorised according to reading index at the end of remedial treatment (in percentages)

Table 7

	Below 0·65	0·65 to below 0·80	0·80 to 1·00	1·00+
Group A (20)	45	55	0	0
Group B (20)	0	25	70	5

The problem of calculating significant factors in cases of reading difficulty

It is probably only by means of individual study that investigators will be able to demonstrate the factors that are significant in cases of reading difficulty. Past investigations have shown that the causation of reading failure is multifactorial. One method of classifying the data from individual cases is to record in tables the presence or absence of relevant factors in each case. When Malmquist (1958) used this method she found that children whose reading performance was markedly inferior to that expected for their mental ages appeared to come mainly from families of low socio-economic status, their parents had had little education, and the children suffered from speech and other defects. In many cases these children had had severe or prolonged illness before coming to school, possessed normal sociability, but lacked persistence, concentration and emotional stability.

Factors considered to be probable causes of reading disability (Y: Yes   N: No)

Table 8

Group A

Case number	Initials	Low intelligence below IQ 85	Poor general physical condition	Defective vision	Defective hearing	Defective speech	Very limited vocabulary	Low social age below SQ 85	Ill-lateralised	Right/left disorientation	Inadequate school methods	Adverse socio-economic background	Poor attendance below 60 per cent	Emotional and personality problems	Low developmental age below 80 quotient	Number of probable causes
1A	L.E.	Y	N	N	N	N	N	Y	N	Y	N	Y	Y	N	Y	6
2A	A.G.	N	N	N	N	Y	N	N	Y	N	N	Y	N	N	Y	4
3A	O.S.	Y	N	N	N	Y	Y	Y	Y	Y	N	Y	N	Y	Y	9
4A	J.P.	Y	N	N	N	Y	Y	Y	Y	Y	N	Y	N	Y	Y	9
5A	D.M.	Y	N	Y	N	N	N	Y	N	Y	N	Y	N	N	Y	6
6A	J.S.	N	N	N	N	N	N	Y	N	Y	N	Y	N	N	Y	4
7A	E.G.	N	N	N	N	N	N	N	N	Y	N	Y	N	N	N	2
8A	D.G.	Y	Y	Y	N	Y	Y	Y	Y	N	N	N	N	Y	Y	9
9A	K.L.	N	Y	N	N	Y	Y	N	Y	Y	N	Y	N	N	Y	6
10A	D.M.	Y	N	N	N	N	Y	Y	N	N	Y	Y	N	N	Y	6
11A	S.G.	Y	N	Y	Y	Y	Y	Y	N	Y	Y	Y	N	Y	Y	11
12A	S.L.	N	N	N	N	N	N	N	N	N	Y	Y	Y	N	N	3
13A	P.D.	N	N	N	N	N	N	N	N	N	N	N	N	N	N	0
14A	A.A.	N	N	N	N	N	Y	Y	N	Y	N	N	N	Y	Y	5
15A	S.B.	Y	Y	Y	Y	N	N	Y	Y	Y	Y	Y	Y	Y	Y	12
16A	I.T.	N	N	N	N	N	N	N	Y	N	N	Y	N	N	N	2
17A	K.R.	Y	N	Y	N	Y	N	Y	N	Y	N	Y	Y	N	Y	8
18A	K.R.	Y	N	N	N	Y	N	Y	N	N	N	Y	Y	N	Y	6
19A	A.L.	N	N	N	N	N	N	N	N	N	Y	Y	N	N	N	2
20A	M.E.	N	N	N	N	N	N	N	N	N	N	Y	Y	Y	N	3
No. of factors		10	3	5	2	8	7	12	7	11	5	17	6	7	13	Total 113

Table 8 has been compiled from factors considered to be contributory causes of reading disability. An attempt was made to ascertain whether the persistent reading failure of Group A was attributable to the cumulative effect of unfavourable characteristics centred in the child, school and home. It was found that the mean number of adverse characteristics for Group A was significantly higher than for Group B. However, a small proportion of Group A had relatively few adverse characteristics.

Table 8 continued

Group B

Case number	Initials	Low intelligence below IQ 85	Poor general physical condition	Defective vision	Defective hearing	Defective speech	Very limited vocabulary	Low social age below SQ 85	Ill-lateralised	Right/left disorientation	Inadequate school methods	Adverse socio-economic background	Poor attendance below 60 per cent	Emotional and personality problems	Low developmental age below 80 quotient	Number of probable causes
1B	W.W.	Y	N	N	N	Y	N	Y	N	N	N	Y	N	N	N	4
2B	S.C.	N	N	N	N	N	N	Y	Y	Y	N	Y	N	N	Y	5
3B	D.L.	Y	N	N	N	Y	N	Y	N	N	N	Y	N	Y	Y	6
4B	N.E.	Y	N	N	N	N	N	Y	N	Y	N	Y	N	N	Y	5
5B	E.O.	Y	Y	Y	N	N	N	Y	N	Y	N	N	N	Y	Y	7
6B	I.U.	N	N	N	N	N	N	N	N	N	N	N	N	N	N	0
7B	M.S.	N	N	N	N	N	N	N	N	N	Y	N	N	N	N	1
8B	G.C.	Y	N	N	N	Y	N	Y	N	Y	N	Y	N	Y	Y	7
9B	E.M.	N	N	N	N	Y	N	N	N	N	N	Y	N	N	N	2
10B	J.D.	N	N	N	N	N	N	N	N	N	N	Y	N	N	N	1
11B	L.B.	Y	N	N	N	Y	N	Y	N	N	N	Y	N	Y	Y	6
12B	J.V.B.	N	N	N	N	N	N	N	N	N	Y	Y	N	N	N	2
13B	D.F.	N	Y	Y	N	Y	N	N	N	N	Y	Y	N	N	N	5
14B	C.L.	N	N	N	N	Y	N	N	Y	N	N	Y	N	N	N	3
15B	D.M.	Y	N	N	N	N	N	N	N	N	N	Y	N	N	N	2
16B	B.L.	N	N	N	N	N	N	N	N	Y	N	Y	N	Y	N	3
17B	P.O.	Y	N	N	N	N	N	Y	N	N	N	Y	N	N	Y	4
18B	D.F.	Y	N	N	N	Y	N	Y	N	Y	N	Y	N	N	Y	6
19B	T.G.	N	N	N	N	N	N	N	Y	N	N	Y	N	N	N	2
20B	J.F.	N	N	N	N	Y	N	N	N	N	N	Y	N	Y	N	3
No. of factors		9	2	2	0	9	0	9	3	6	3	17	0	6	8	Total 74

and a similar proportion of Group B had several. It has been concluded that this approach has its limitations and that the reasons for inhibited reading progress possibly lie in the complexity of the individual attributes, environment, etc., which would be better studied in each individual case history.

The remedial methods adopted

It is frequently maintained by educationists that remedial teaching is good first teaching; that remedial methods are in essence the same as the methods adopted in the successful teaching of so-called normal children. They differ only in that they are applied with greater flexibility and more discrimination and that remedial methods are based upon normal classroom practices—the things a good teacher ought to do. All agree that remedial teachers should have confidence in themselves, a sympathetic understanding of the child, an appreciation of the limitation of the child, and a precise knowledge and understanding of the reading materials available and used at different levels of ability. Educationists agree that different teachers attain different degrees of success with different methods. In planning his reading programme, each teacher should consider his own personality and his approach with the class. If the approach is good and the child can relax then the atmosphere created will enable the child to experience success and failure in his stride.

Many remedial methods used today follow the suggestions of Fernald (1943), Monroe (1946), Gates (1947), Schonell (1958), Burt (1950) and others. Schonell advocated an eclectic method based upon the early forms of remedial work in the USA. This method is a combination of 'look and say', sentence and phonic work. Children are encouraged to memorise a poem. They then 'read' the poem from memory and this, it appears, gives the children confidence to tackle words. A child learns the words linked with a topic of interest before eventually writing about the topic. This method includes graded materials including picture cards, tracing cards, memorising, etc. Phonics are introduced later. Many teachers have used their own adaptations of Schonell's method.

The visual-auditory-kinaesthetic-tactile modes of learning (Fernald, 1943) have been successfully used by teachers for over sixty years. They are based on an experience or interest approach.

Roberts (1960) carried out a study of motivation in remedial reading. He carried out an experiment with three groups of children using three different methods:

Method A—The basis of motivation was curiosity and creative drive, using an adaptation of Fernald's method.

Method B—The motivation depended on gregariousness. The method was based upon those of Gates and Schonell. It consisted of (i) a word enrichment programme; (ii) co-operative reading; (iii) individual reading; and (iv) incidental phonic analysis.

Method C—The basis for motivation was competition. Monroe's basic approach was followed but her method was not used in its entirety.

Roberts found that Method A was superior to the other two methods as a means of teaching reading to retarded readers between the ages of nine and eleven years.

For many years the merits of 'look and say' and phonics have been discussed. Many people have advocated one method to the absolute exclusion of the other. Many experiments have proved that the differing abilities of teachers to apply different methods have led to inconclusive and confusing results. Vernon (1957) emphasises the impossibility of assessing exactly the skill of the teachers who employ these methods.

Vernon (1960) says that experiments comparing different methods are not carried out for a sufficient period of time. His criticism is that claims are frequently made for one method or another because improvement in reading has been greater on average than when another method was used. But when the children are tested after a follow-up investigation, there is frequently no significant difference in achievement between the two groups. Williams (1965) has also emphasised the many problems involved in the experimental comparison of teaching methods. Collins (1961) found the same problems when he used follow-up tests two or three years later; and so did Lovell et al. (1962, 1963).

Many educators have shown their concern about the stage at which phonics should be taught. Others are concerned with the priority of phonics over other methods. Schonell (1945) maintains that it is inadvisable to introduce phonics at too early an age. He suggests that a child should have reached a level of maturity and mental readiness over and above that required for beginning reading before he is ready for phonic training. Bruce (1964) supports the view of Schonell. He studied the ability shown by children at different levels of mental development for the task of making simple phonetic analysis of spoken words. His results suggest that a mental level of 7+ is required to overcome the various difficulties involved. But Flesch (1955), an American investigator, maintains that a great deal of retardation in reading is due to the neglect of phonic methods. He is supported in this country by several educationists including Daniels and Diack (1954, 1956). Their reading scheme, *The Royal Road Readers,* is firmly based on the phonic method. Some educationists, including Durrell (1956) and Fries (1963), advocate the teaching of the letter names as part of early teaching of reading. Malmquist (1958) suggests a form of compromise. She says that the beginner should learn as soon as possible to recognise the most visual word patterns in their entirety, even if he has been trained by the phonic method. She maintains that children who begin to learn to read by 'look and say'—'whole sentence' method should, on the other hand, be taught, as soon as they have learned about a hundred word patterns, 'the technique of reproducing the values of the sounds of the printed or written signs, one by one in the right order from left to right, and to combine them so as to form words or phrases'.

It has been the opinion of many teachers that because many poor readers verbalise, oral response in learning to read is detrimental to reading progress. An interesting study was carried out in the USA by McNeil and Keisler (1963) to discover whether kindergarten children taught by programmed reading materials which require the saying of words and sentences aloud would achieve greater skills in reading than children taught by the same programmed materials with no instruction to speak out loud. The superiority of the oral responders was significant when based on the average difference between matched pairs.

It is essential for a remedial teacher of reading to review and scrutinise the methods of teaching used in his remedial classes. It was found that, during the investigation, one was unable to cater for individual needs in exactly the same manner every year. Even though the method had been similar in certain cases, this did not mean that the manner of approach was the same.

It is essential that reading failures encounter words in their reading which they will be using frequently in their natural conversation and in their written work. Vernon (1948) found in his investigation that the speech vocabulary of five-year-olds

191

and the vocabulary content of Infant Readers showed clearly that there were far too many words in early readers that were not connected with the natural conversation of children. (Many of the books studied by Vernon are still used today.) Many words commonly used by five-year-olds in their conversations were not found in any of the seventeen books examined. In many of the phonic readers up to forty per cent of the printed vocabulary was outside the natural conversation of children. Bernstein (1961) has also emphasised that one should take the level of speech of working class children into consideration when tackling the problems of reading and writing failure. Briggs (1966) also brought out this point in his address to the 1966 Conference on the Backward Child.

For those children requiring pre-reading work, a wide range of activities was used to enrich the children's experience, encourage the growth of language, and allow the children to relax and feel at home in a happy and friendly atmosphere. Emphasis was placed on the building up of a functional language background so that the children would know the meaning of most words that would occur in their early reading activities. The general approach adopted was divided into three parts. First, a varied and stimulating programme including art, plays, stories, talks, use of the tape recorder, and pictures in order to develop a functional language background; second, to encourage the recognition of words and short sentences in meaningful wholes; third, to bring together the meanings of familiar and unfamiliar words in order to recreate them as ideas in writing.

In the case of all those children who were not reading their first primer, each child was helped to make his first reader. These books consisted of pictures showing the individual's own interests and activities and one or two words to add to their meaning. These words were written in bold clear script for the child to copy. An adequate repetition of these words was also given. Additional reading apparatus and materials were continually at hand and were used throughout the remedial treatment. When the child was ready for his first reader, then he was also prepared to read many of the words contained in the reader because of the previous activities. Use was also made of a tape recorder and headphones. The child was allowed to sit, listen and follow the reading of the story without distracting the rest of the group. Incidental phonic games and activities were used from the beginning. Early phonic training consisted of using those words already known to the child. Plenty of phonic apparatus was available but the children found particular pleasure in playing the games contained in Stott's *Programmed Reading Kit* (Holmes McDougall, 1962). Sandpaper and plastic letters were used together with a sand tray.

An attempt was made to make remedial teaching a total approach to reading failure. Creative and therapeutic activities were adopted as much as possible but full benefit could not be derived from this approach because of the limited amount of time available for each group. A considerable amount of writing was done throughout the period of remedial treatment. This writing helped the children whether they were at the early stages of reading or whether they were fairly well established on a reading scheme (e.g. *Ladybird Key Words Reading Scheme*).

Examples of reading materials designed for the slow readers

A large proportion of the reading material used by the children was devised by the author. Frequently, material was specifically devised for individual children. It was not unusual to find that commercially-produced material was not relevant to the needs of the individual child.

The approach adopted and further examples of materials may be seen in Chapter 3, *The Initial Stages,* but a more detailed study of approaches and the use of reading materials may be found in two books published by Evans Brothers: *Aids to Reading* and *Phonics and the Teaching of Reading*. Much of the material devised to help those children lacking the necessary tools to unlock unknown words has now been incorporated in three phonic workbooks published by Nelson under the title *Moving on with Reading*. These books combine a basic sight vocabulary with an incidental phonic approach. Further practical suggestions may be obtained from two books published by Evans in the *Education in Action* series: *Beginning Reading* and *Reading with Phonics*.

The following are further examples of the materials used with the slow readers throughout the investigation. One will notice that particular emphasis has been placed on exercises involving phonic work. This highlights one of the main weaknesses exhibited by the children.

193

Find the right word.
Write the word in the box

	bat cat hat	
	call fall ball	
	cap tap map	
	fell well bell	
	how cow now	
	hug rug mug	
	bag flag rag	

Find the right word.
Write the word in the box.

4.

	goat boat coat	
	train rain chain	
	town crown town	
	snail sail tail	
	paw saw straw	
	head bread spread	
	sweet feet beet	

Yes and No Cards

Is the dog under the table?

Are the apples on the table?

Does the cat jump on the box ?

Is the balloon up in the air?

Is this an aeroplane?

Programmed remedial reading exercises

One approach to remedial teaching was to prepare a series of programmed remedial reading exercises. Programmed learning is an attempt to make learning as easy as possible. The material is broken down into a series of short steps. Programmed reading material demands constant activity on the part of the child because it involves a constant interchange between it and the child. The child is informed immediately of the success or failure of his response. He is able to use the material at his own pace and there is not the same time lag as he would experience in the normal classroom situation where he has to wait for the teacher to attend to him.

The teacher must consider whether the content of the material holds the child's interest and whether the child is notified of his mistakes and is able to correct himself. The teacher must also consider whether the written work involved is suitable for the child and reinforces his learning.

The construction of the programmed reading material

Simple programmed reading material may be made using the word-cue/picture-prompt idea. Divide the pages of an exercise

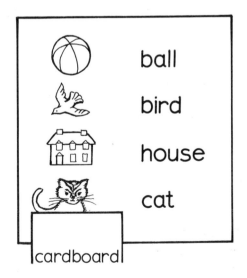

book into halves. Turn to the first page and at the top right-hand corner print a word, e.g. 'bat'. On the reverse side paste a picture of a bat or use a simple line drawing. The picture gives immediate reinforcement to the response. The child works along the top of the book to the back, turns the book over, and works to the front. Confirmation of each response is in the form of a picture on the reverse side of each page.

Prepare a card with pictures or drawings on one side and corresponding words on the other. The child studies the pictures and words and later he covers up the pictures with a strip of cardboard. The child attempts each word and moves the cardboard down to reveal the corresponding picture and is informed of the success or failure of his response.

The following is a selection of programmed reading worksheets used with the children. These were prepared on a master sheet and then cyclostyled using a Banda machine.

1. SIGHT WORDS	Here is a		ball house $\rangle$ · · · ·
house	Here is a		door cat $\rangle$ · · · ·
door	Here is a		bird cat $\rangle$ · · · ·
cat	Here is a		ball dog $\rangle$ · · · ·
ball	Here is a		house boat $\rangle$ · · · ·
boat			

2. SIGHT WORDS				
	Here is the	🍵	cup hat	>····
cup	I see the	🎩	table hat	>····
hat	Here is the	🐦	bird bat	>····
bird	I see the	🪑	horse table	>····
table	Here is the	🏏	bat bed	>····
bat				

5. INITIAL SOUNDS				
	I see the		pan man fan	>····
man	This is a		bin pin tin	>····
tin	We see the		hat bat cat	>····
bat	Here is the		hen pen ten	>····
pen	We can see the	☀	sun bun gun	>····
sun				

199

6. SIGHT WORDS AND INITIAL SOUNDS		
	Here is a	b _ _
bed	This is my	d _ _
dog	I see the	b _ _ _
boat	This is my	h _ _ _ _
house	Here is the	t _ _ _ _
table		

7. SIGHT WORDS AND INITIAL SOUNDS		
	I like the	b _ _ _
bird	Here is the	h _ _ _ _
horse	I have a	h _ _
hat	We can see the	f _ _ _
fish	We like this	c _ _
car		

8. INITIAL SOUNDS	I have a		rat bat cat → · · · ·
bat	Here is a		leg peg beg → · · · ·
peg	We can see the		pig fig big → · · · ·
pig	This is my		rag bag wag → · · · ·
bag	I have a		pot dot hot → · · · ·
pot			

11. FINAL SOUNDS	This is a		man map mat → · · · ·
mat	I have the		cub cup cut → · · · ·
cup	I like this		pin pit pig → · · · ·
pig	This is my		peg pen pet → · · · ·
pen	Here is the		pod pot pop → · · · ·
pot			

14. MIDDLE VOWEL SOUNDS	I see the		pit pot pet	→ . . . .
pot	This is my		pin pan pen	→ . . . .
pen	Here is the		bin bun ban.	→ . . . .
bin	We see the		cut cot cat	→ . . . .
cot	Here is the		fun fin fan	→ . . . .
fan				

17. CONSONANT BLENDS AND DIGRAPHS	The pig has a big	spout snout shout	→ . . . .
snout	We use a rope to	slip skip ship	→ . . . .
skip	I do not like	shakes snakes stakes	→ . . . .
snakes	I have a bag of	sheets greets sweets	→ . . . .
sweets	We use cards to play	clap slap snap	→ . . . .
snap			

20. VOWEL DIGRAPHS	We eat with a sp__n	ou oa oo
spoon	We put a cup on a s__cer	ai ay au
saucer	We sailed up the river in a b__t	ou ow oa
boat	We wear shoes on our f__t	ea ee ei
feet	The cat has a long t__l	ai ou ea
tail		

25. STORIES	One day we went for a ____	walk talk chalk
walk	We saw two boys having a ____	might light fight
fight	Tom jumped on Ben's ____	sack back rack
back	Ben fell to the ____	round pound ground
ground	Tom ran down the ____	sweet street sleet
street		

These worksheets have been selected from a programmed series in order to show examples of the form of progression adopted. The child uses a piece of cardboard and places this under the first line. The answer is covered up. The child can check his response by moving the cardboard to the next line. The correct answer is found in the left-hand column. Children may be told either to underline or circle what they consider is the correct answer, or print in the word where this is necessary.

The class reading programme

The question continually being asked by teachers was:'What follow-up work should I carry out with those children coming to you for extra tuition?' Fortunately, because of the excellent co-operation existing between the investigator and the head-teachers and staff of the schools visited by the investigator, he was able to discuss an appropriate approach to the teaching of reading in the classes where his pupils were to be found.

I put forward a suggestion for a reading programme that would involve all the children in the classes so that not only would the slow readers benefit but so would the other children—in other words, a programme that would cater for individual rates of growth in reading and individual interests, a programme that would cater for the needs of the slow readers and, at the same time, extend the better readers.

I planned a method of reading whereby each child selected his own reading material—reading material that interested him. It was hoped that the slow reader would be motivated by interest and progress at his own individual rate of reading growth. When one adopts this approach, there is always the danger that the interest of the child may be extremely narrow so the teacher and I had to guide certain children along the right road, hoping to widen their interests.

I wished to provide for the slow readers reading material that catered for the words they used in everyday speech and the words they would use in their writing. I wished to break away from the traditional early reading books that involve a restricted, meaning-less vocabulary for these children and for many other children in the class. I believe that we must ask the questions: 'Are the reading schemes on the market today appropriate for many of our children and, in particular, are they appropriate for the slow reader?'

Who are Peter and Jane? Who are Janet and John? Surely these characters are far removed from the reality of many slower children's experiences.

Should one stop using the 'make a book' approach as soon as the child has started on the 'reading road?' Why should we not allow the slow reader to continue to write his own reading books? These books would refer to his way of life and his culture rather than the 'foreign' way of life and strange culture of many of the characters in certain published reading schemes. So let us continue to use the child's language. His words will have meaning because they refer to his own way of life.

These slower children experienced the problem of knowing how to put words together to express ideas. We are all well aware of the fact that this ability must be achieved first in speech. Another problem for these children is to have something to say and the importance of oral activity cannot be over-emphasised. The written work of these children should be about things the children have done or seen, or for a specific purpose which these children fully understand. Many of them had limited experiences and it became necessary to arrange morning and afternoon jaunts and other school visits. If writing is to be effective writing then the child must feel that there is a need or purpose behind what he is going to write.

The imposition of certain cultures contained in several reading schemes on some children in our schools has a detrimental effect. The world of many characters in these schemes is far removed from the real world most of my children live in. What a glorious Disneyland Peter and Jane live in. What a wonderful world of colour. What beautiful clothes they always appear to be wearing. What wonderful gardens they play in. What bright and dazzling colours are used on the picture pages—what a contrast to the drab reality of my children's environments. Can we honestly say that many of our slow learners who come from poor socio-economic environments live the same kind of lives as Peter and Jane and other characters portrayed in other reading schemes? Are the activities, interests, etc. those of many of our 'deprived' children? Is there mention of parents' interest in 'The Club', 'Bingo', 'The Dogs', 'The United', 'On telly last night', etc.?

If words have intense meanings for children then they will learn these quite quickly. How often do we find that infant children learn the word 'space-ship' or even 'astronaut' and do not learn shorter but rather 'mundane' words. If we are to improve

205

the language, reading and writing of these children, we must, first of all, accept what they have to say in their own language and base our teaching of reading on their vocabulary. We must encourage these children to talk freely and provide them with the opportunities to express themselves in dramatic activities, painting, modelling, etc.

Many of these children have failed to read in the past because the reading they encountered was completely divorced from the reality of their own circumstances. They were never given the opportunity to appreciate that reading could be a very personal thing and very relevant to their lives. The environment of the school and the child's classroom should compensate for the deprivation many of these children suffer. But the aim should be to bring in the reality of the outside world.

So for the follow-up work with my slow readers, I provided a wide range of reading materials. With the help of the class teachers, I adopted a colour code for books for all the children in the classes so that they were guided to books and materials appropriate to their reading age. The children were given a free choice but, with teacher-guidance, some soon began to appreciate the books that they could read and those that were too difficult. I arranged the books in categories to cater for a wide range of interests. The number of books was increased over a period of time and 'swops' were carried out between classes to ensure a wider range of choice. Eventually a substantial range of books was provided. During this period, teachers continued to give the slow readers as many opportunities as possible to express themselves in various activities and writing. The writing included stories, report, etc. The whole of the class participated in these activities.

Record cards were very carefully kept throughout the period and it was interesting to note how many more books were read as a result of this form of individualised reading. This approach increased the amount of reading and writing for all children and, over a period of one year, there was a significant increase in reading accuracy, fluency and comprehension. As a result of adopting individualised reading, it was noted that the slower children's attempts at writing their own stories and describing events began to improve and there was an increase in the various activities arising from their reading of books of their own choice.

Concluding thoughts

The most important implication for teaching from our knowledge of child growth and development comes from the fact of individuality. Each child is a unique entity. Probably many of the children in Group B were on the verge of reading, and the progress which they made would have occured without remedial treatment. It is possible that the period of remedial treatment coincided with the natural period of readiness reflected by the rate of growth of certain children, but, in the case of others, this was to come later.

Particular concern has been shown regarding the adverse socioeconomic background of the vast majority of the research sample. Many of these children need remedies that are social rather than extra teaching in remedial classes. Some of the homes were quite shocking. A considerable amount of research has been carried out into the effects of adverse home environment on the scholastic progress of children. There is general agreement that these effects can be very detrimental indeed in the cases of many children. It is probably true that the lower the intellectual ability of the child, the greater the problem of overcoming the effects of a deprived home environment (Curry, 1962). There is considerable evidence in professional literature that the level of intellectual functioning can be suppressed because of adverse home environments.

Today, research is inclined to contradict the idea that intelligence is fixed at conception. There now appears to be a growing body of opinion which suggests that the development of intelligence is determined by experience, and emphasis is placed particularly on early experience. In order that a child may develop intellectually, he should have the freedom to experiment and find out things for himself. He needs adults to answer his questions and to ask him questions in order that his language will develop. In this respect, a child needs parents who will talk to him, read to him, surround him with words, even if he is too young to understand them. When a child lives in an adverse environment he rarely has the stimulation mentioned above. Such deprived children may benefit from being exposed to the stimulation that is missing in their own homes, if they can be reached at an early age.

However good the provision of schools, teachers and facilities, and however enlightened the methods of teaching, nothing is accomplished if the pupils are not present. Frequently the main cause of absence from school is the apathy of the parents.

Early ascertainment is required in order that teachers are made aware of children who can be regarded as 'educational risks' as early as possible in the child's schooling. In order to do this, it would become necessary for ascertainment during pre-school years. It is appreciated that the earlier a child is examined, the more difficult is the accurate assessment of his potential, but this does not mean that, in many cases, we should wait for a child to fail before taking action. If a child is to be ascertained before the start of his primary education, then this could be done in nursery schools. An 'at risk' register (in the medical sense) could be the basis for early ascertainment of intellectual impairment. Nursery units could be used to alleviate the burdens of mothers with large families who, for various reasons, are unable to give the necessary care and attention to their children. Certain children could be given the stimulation that is missing in the home by putting them into nursery units.

Many children who are backward enter the infant school. Many of them will, after six years, fail to cope with our present primary school set-up. In an attempt to 'make' these children readers before they enter the junior school, the infant teacher may 'force' them into superficial progress. When the children enter junior school, they are placed at the bottom half of the class containing those children with the lowest ability. Probably, for the rest of their junior school years, they will fail to keep pace and will eventually leave for the secondary school three to four years retarded. There is an urgent need for all schools, in a particular area, to liaise with each other and attempt to co-ordinate their efforts to make full use of a primary system that frequently neglects those children in need of the greatest attention. After all, each school has the same problem.

The class teacher has the responsibility for obtaining all the information on the individual child that is relevant to his reading development. But it is frequently impossible to adopt the correct approach for each child when the teacher has the task of starting thirty-six children upon the most difficult of all tasks. Under these conditions, the ability to accumulate sufficient information about each child and therefore to be able to assess how his learning may best be directed is frequently beyond the capacity of the teacher. But even when faced with these problems, the teacher must attempt to cater for the children in the best way possible. A large class should be divided into smaller groups by providing a wide variety of reading and practical material, and by using every opportunity for observation that offers itself during the day. A certain amount of attention can be given to the needs of individual children even in the large classes.

Frequently, adequate provision for the child is wasted by the lack of liaison between teachers. Problems are created in the lower classes of primary schools as a result of lack of attention to individual differences in children's pre-reading activities and in their readiness to read. A disregard of these individual differences frequently results in initial failure to read, which could lead the child to think of himself as a non-reader and this may persist for many years. There are large individual differences between children when it comes to the age at which they begin to read. In a good environment where the child has picture books shown to him, stories and rhymes read to him, and where the adult conversation around him is stimulating, readiness for reading follows quite naturally and quite incidentally. When a child is ready to start reading, he will show an increased interest in his picture books and in having stories read to him, and will probably hold up a book and pretend to read.

It is essential that the class teacher provides a suitable range of reading material if children are to become successful readers in all situations. A class of thirty-six will warrant a very wide range of suitable reading material because it must be remembered that each individual child will require a good variety of material.

Many parents are liable to blame the teacher for a child's lack of progress in reading. However, they will very quickly take the praise for their children when they show exceptional progress in any aspect of school work. People who criticise the teacher do not appreciate the many factors that influence a child's success and, in particular, that reading is a part of a continuous growing process. A teacher may be very experienced and proficient, she may have the most excellent reading programme, but still certain children will not read as well as the majority.

It is hoped that this investigation has answered some of the questions concerning reading ability. It has been seen that many factors can be in operation and these factors may defeat, for a while, the best efforts of the best teacher, but it is only by knowing the child as an individual that a teacher can understand his problems and give him the best possible chance of progressing according to his rate of all-round growth.

Appendices

Appendix A

Factors found in the research cases

Factors	Group A (No. 20) %	Group B (No. 20) %
Home circumstances		
Foster home	0	5
Step-parent	0	5
Death of parent	0	5
Absence of parent/work	15	10
Illegitimacy	0	5
Parental health		
Poor health	20	20
Emotional strain	40	35
Parental attitudes		
Weak/inadequate	55	40
Over-protective	10	10
Harsh	10	10
Occupations		
Skilled worker	10	30
Unskilled	80	70
Unemployed	10	0
Mother working/part time	10	10
Mother working/full time	30	20

Factors	Group A	Group B
	(No. 20)	(No. 20)
	%	%

Atmosphere of home

Sibling rivalry	20	30
Friction between parents	50	35
Violence	10	10
Drunkeness	20	10
Delinquency	20	15
Misdirection of recreational activities	70	55

Material conditions

Family size/living space

Good	10	0
Above average	5	5
Average	15	10
Below average	35	25
Very poor	35	60

Educational background

Parental interest shown	15	20
Interruption of schooling because of poor attendance	30	0
Unsuitable teaching methods	25	15
Poor teacher-child relations	25	20

Position of child in family

Oldest	10	20
Between	65	65
Youngest	15	10
Only	10	5

Factors	Group A	Group B
	(No. 20)	(No. 20)
	%	%

Health of child

Good general health	30	55
Fair general health	55	35
Poor general health	15	10

Specific defects

Vision	25	10
Hearing	10	0
Ears, nose, throat	10	0
Speech (present and/or past)	40	45
Asthma	5	0
Enuresis	10	0
Poor health: pre-school years	50	35

Mental level

Dull (IQ 70–84)	50	45
Low average (IQ 85–89)	15	10
Average (IQ 90–109)	35	45

Emotional and personality adjustment

Above average	10	20
Normal	50	50
Below normal	20	25
Well below normal	15	5

Social maturity

Above average	0	0
Average	25	45
Below average	15	10
Well below average	60	45

215

Appendix B

Further useful information on the teaching of reading

Cambridge Institute of Education, Shaftesbury Avenue, Cambridge.
Information on reading schemes, i.e. *Trends in Reading Schemes* and *Reading Schemes: their Emphases and their Interchangeability.*

The Centre for the Teaching of Reading, 29 Eastern Avenue, Reading RG1 5RJ.
Information on many aspects of teaching reading including reading schemes for primary schools, reading schemes for slow learners, reading tests, reading methods, information leaflets on various aspects of reading and a check list of basic sounds.

Child Guidance Service, 12 Grange Road, West Bromwich.
Reading schemes for slow learners.

Derbyshire Education Committee, School Library Service.
A selected list of books for less able children in primary schools (and another list for secondary schools).

Kent Education Committee.
Books and publications recommended for use with dull and backward children.

Leeds Child Guidance Service.
Books and apparatus for backward readers in the primary school.

National Book League, 7 Albemarle Street, London W1.
Help in Reading. Books for the teacher of backward children and for pupils backward in reading.

217

School Library Books.
Books for Young People (School Library Association).
Four to Fourteen National Book League (CUP).
Primary School Library Books (School Library Association).
Intent upon Reading (Brockhampton Press).
Tales out of School (Heinemann).
The Use of Books (DES).
The School Library (DES).
Literature and the Young Child (Longman).

The United Kingdom Reading Association (UKRA), Hon. Gen. Sec., 63 Laurel Grove, Sunderland SR2 9EE.
The Association publishes a journal once a term *(Reading)* and a news letter, and has produced many books on reading including reports on conferences and a series of monographs of interest to teachers of reading.

University of Leeds Institute of Education.
Information on reading schemes and materials in children's learning.

West Sussex Psychological Service, Education Department, County Hall, Chichester.
A number of pamphlets including *Reading Schemes, Phonics, Assessment of Reading Ability* and *Teaching Non-Readers*.

Relevant journals

English in Education The National Association of Teachers of English.
Forward Trends Guild of Teachers of Backward Children, Minster Chambers, Southwell, Nottinghamshire.
Reading The United Kingdom Reading Association (UKRA), Hon. Gen. Sec., 63 Laurel Grove, Sunderland SR2 9EE.
Special Education The Association for Special Education, Gen. Sec., 19 Hamilton Road, Wallasey.
Teachers World Evans Brothers Ltd., Montague House, Russell Square, London WC1B 5BX.
Various Publications The College of Special Education, 85 Newman Street, London W1.

The use of tapes

Audio Reading Aid H. C. Gillard, 3 Stafford Road, Petersfield.
The Clifton Audio/Visual Reading Programme ESA, Pinnacles, Harlow, Essex.
The English Colour Code System Centre for Learning Disabilities, 86 Newman Street, London W1.
Ladybird Key Words Reading Scheme Wills and Hepworth, Loughborough, Leicestershire.
Listening to Sounds E. J. Arnold, Butterley Street, Leeds 10.
McKee Readers, Ladybird Key Words Reading Scheme and Phonic Tapes G. Greenwood, 67 Heath Farm Road, Norton, Stourbridge, Worcestershire.
Sound Discrimination, Listening Tapes, Phonic Tapes, Matching Tapes, Sentence Building Remedial Supply Company, Dixon Street, Wolverhampton.

Materials to assist language development

Peabody Language Development Kits NFER, The Mere, Upton Park, Slough.
Pictures and Words Blackie and Son Limited, Bishopbriggs, Glasgow.
The SRA Language Development Programme SRA, Reading Road, Henley-on-Thames, Oxfordshire.
The 'Talkmore' Project E. J. Arnold, Butterley Street, Leeds 10.

Audio visual aids

Automatic Filmstrip Projector Bell and Howell, Alperton House, Bridgewater Road, Wembley, Middlesex.
Language Master Bell and Howell.
Packette Tape Recorder E. J. Arnold.
Reading Accelerator SRA.
The Stillitron Stillit Books Limited, 72 New Bond Street, London W1.

Filmstrips and slides

Common Ground Longman House, Burnt Mill, Harlow, Essex.

Educational Production Limited East Ardsley, Wakefield, Yorkshire.

Slides: CI Audio Visual Limited 6 Rosemont Road, Hampstead, London NW3.

Sound Services Limited Industrial Aids Department, Kingston Road, Merton Park, London SW19.

Weston Woods Studios Limited PO Box 2, Henley-on-Thames, Oxfordshire.

A selected reading list

Aids to Reading (Evans Brothers) J. M. Hughes.

Backwardness in Reading (CUP) M. D. Vernon.

Colour Story Reading (Nelson) J. K. Jones.

Dr Montessori's Own Handbook (Heinemann) M. Montessori.

Dyslexia: A Guide for Teachers and Parents University of Aston, Gosta Green, Birmingham B4 7ET.

The English Colour Code Programmed Reading Course (NSMHC) D. Mosely.

Modern Innovations in the Teaching of Reading (ULP) D. and L. Moyle.

The Montessori Method (Heinemann) M. Montessori.

On Helping the Dyslexic Child (Methuen) T. R. Miles.

Phonics and the Teaching of Reading (Evans Brothers) J. M. Hughes.

Practical Reading (Evans Brothers) J. Webster.

Reading and its Difficulties—a Psychological Study (CUP) M. D. Vernon.

Reading and the Dyslexic Child (Souvenir Press) R. Crosby and R. Liston.

Reading in Primary Schools (Routledge and Kegan Paul) G. R. Roberts.

Reading Readiness (ULP) J. Downing and J. Thackray.

Reading and Remedial Reading (Routledge and Kegan Paul) A. E. Tansley.

Reading—Which Approach? (ULP) V. Southgate and G. R. Roberts.

220

Reading, Writing and Talking (A and C Black) J. Dean.
A Remedial Reading Method (Methuen) C. A. J. Moxon.
The Teaching of Reading (Ward Lock Educational) D. Moyle.
Words in Colour (Educational Explorers) C. Gattegno.
Words Your Children Use (Burke) R. Edwards and V. Gibbon.

Several publications on reading by Department and Faculty of Education, UC Swansea—obtainable from Singleton Bookshop, Singleton Park, Swansea.

Phonic materials

Basic Reading Series (SRA)
Beacon Readers (Ginn)
First Sounds (Gibson)
Fun with Phonics (Cambridge Art Pub.)
Gay Way (Macmillan)
Get Reading Right (Gibson)
Happy Families (Macdonald)
Moving on with Reading (Nelson)
Patterns of Sound (Chartwell Press)
Phonic Programmes for Autobates Machine
Phonic Word Games (SRA)
Remedial Refresher Cards (Gibson)
Royal Road Readers (Chatto and Windus)
Six Phonic Workbooks (Ginn)
Soundabout Phonic Cards (Hart-Davis)
Sounding and Blending (Gibson)
Sounds Right (Gibson)
Sounds and Words (ULP)
Sound Sense (E. J. Arnold)
Step up and Read (ULP)
Stott's Programmed Reading Kit (Holmes McDougall)
The Swansea Test of Phonic Skills (Blackwell)
Tackling New Words (ESA)
Word Games (Gibson)
Word Study Kit (Bell and Howell) For use with the Language Master.

Books for children with reading difficulties (RA—reading age; IA—interest age)

Active Reading Series (Ginn) RA 6–9 years; IA secondary.
Adult Readers (Readers Digest)
Adventures in Life (Wheaton) RA 7½–9 years; IA 9–14 years
Adventures in Reading (OUP) RA 5+ years
Adventures in Space (Hart-Davis) RA 7+ years
Ben Books (Longman) RA 6+ years
Booster Books (Heinemann) RA 7½–9 years; IA 11–15 years
Burgess Readers (ULP) RA 8–9½ years; IA 10–14 years
Challenge Readers (Holmes McDougall) RA 6–9 years; IA 9–12 years
Clearway Readers (I.T.A.)
Cowboy Sam Books (E. J. Arnold) RA 6½–8 years; IA 7–11 years
Data Books (Schofield & Sims) RA 7+ years; IA up to secondary
Dolphin Books (ULP) RA 6+ years
Downing Readers (I.T.A.)
Dragon Readers (E. J. Arnold) RA 6–8 years; IA 8–14 years
Far and Near Books (W & R Chambers) RA 7–9 years; IA 10–15 years
The Ginger Books (Ward Lock) 6+ years
Griffin Readers (E. J. Arnold) RA 6–8 years; IA 8–14 years
Inner Ring Books (Benn) RA 7+ years; IA 11–15 years
Interest Books (Warne) RA 7+ years
Jet Books (Jonathan Cape) RA 9+ years; IA 11–15 years
Micky Books (Holmes McDougall) RA 8–9½ years; IA 9–14 years
Mike and Mandy Readers (Nelson) RA 6–8½ years; IA 8–12 years
Modern Reading (ULP) RA 6–8 years; IA 10–14 years
Nippers (Macmillan) RA 6+ years
Onward Readers (Cassell) RA 6+ years
Oxford Colour Reading Books (OUP) RA 6–9 years; IA 8–13 years
Pathfinder Books (Oliver & Boyd) RA 7+; IA up to secondary
Racing to Read (E. J. Arnold) RA 5–7½ years; IA 7–11 years
Rescue Readers (Ginn) RA 6–8 years; IA 7–13 years
Royal Road Readers (Chatto & Windus) RA 5½+ years
Sound Sense (E. J. Arnold) RA 6+ years; IA up to secondary
Step up and Read (ULP) RA 6–8½ years; IA 9–13 years
Story Path to Reading (Blackie) RA 7+ years; IA up to secondary
Joan Tate Books (Heinemann) RA 8+ years; IA up to secondary
Teenage Twelve (Gibson) RA 7+ years; IA 9–13 years
Tempo Books (Longman) RA 6½–8½ years; IA 9–13 years

Trend (Ginn)
Topliners (Macmillan)
Wild West Readers (Wheaton) RA 7+ years; IA up to secondary
Working World Series (Cassells) slow secondary school readers

Other reading materials

Breakthrough to Literacy (Longman)
Reading Workshop (Ward Lock Educational)
Wordmaster Major (Macdonald)

A selection of basic reading material

E. J. Arnold & Son Ltd
Snappy Snap
Shape Sorting
Picture Word Charts
Spellmaster
Photo Puzzles

ESA Ltd
ESA Picture Lotto
Flannelgraph Crossword
Card Picture Dominoes
ESA Jigsaws (on wood)

James Galt & Co Ltd
Phonic Word Jigsaws
Rhymo
Picture Word Lotto
Phonic Self Teacher
Key Words Self Teaching Cards
Phonic Practice Cards
Self Checking Phonic Alphabet
Double Dominoes
Find-a-Pair
Early Reading Jigsaws
Flannelgraph Phonic Reading Set

Robert Gibson & Sons Ltd
Word Games
Tear-off Picture and Word Pads
Sounding and Blending
Sounds Right

Thomas Hope & Sankey Hudson Ltd
Child Guidance Magnetic Alphabet Boards
Scrabble for Juniors and full-size game

Philip & Tacey Ltd
Chelsea Alphabet Chart and Pictorial Symbols
Chelsea Alphabet Cellograph Symbols
Groundwork Key Words and Pictures
Groundwork Key Word Coloured Gummed Stamps
Renown Individual Picture and Word Matching Cards
My Book of Word Families
Family Cellograph Materials
Chameleon Street Picture Making Outfit

Remedial Supply Company
Familiar Situations
Stories without Words
The Reading Cards
Tapes with Work Materials

Visigraph Ltd
Flannelgraph Phonic Kit and other reading materials

Publishers

Edward Arnold, 25 Hill Street, London W1X 8LL.
E. J. Arnold & Son Ltd., Butterley Street, Leeds 10.
Bell & Howell, Alperton House, Bridgewater Road, Wembley, Middlesex.
Ernest Benn, Sovereign Way, Tonbridge, Kent.
A. & C. Black, 4 Soho Square, London W1V 6AD.
Blackie & Son Ltd., Bishopbriggs, Glasgow G64 2N2.
Basil Blackwell & Mott Ltd., 108 Cowley Road, Oxford OX4 1JF

Brockhampton Press Ltd., Salisbury Road, Leicester LE1 7QS.

Burke Publishing Co. Ltd., 14 John Street, London WC1N 2EJ.

Jonathan Cape Ltd., 30 Bedford Square, London WC1B 3EL.

Cassell & Co. Ltd., 35 Red Lion Square, London WC1.

W. & R. Chambers Ltd., 11 Thistle Street, Edinburgh 2.

Geoffrey Chapman Ltd., 35 Red Lion Square, London WC1.

Chatto & Windus Ltd., 40–42 William IV Street, London WC2N 4DF.

Collins Ltd., 14 St. James Place, London SW1.

Common Ground Ltd., Longman House, Burnt Mill, Harlow, Essex.

Cuisenaire Co. Ltd., 40 Silver Street, Reading, Berks.

Educational Productions Ltd., East Ardsley, Wakefield, Yorks.

Educational Supply Association, Pinnacles, Harlow, Essex.

Evans Brothers Ltd., Montague House, Russell Square, London WC1B 5BX.

James Galt & Co. Ltd., Brookfields Road, Cheadle SK8 2PN.

Robert Gibson & Sons Ltd., 17 Fitzroy Place, Glasgow.

Ginn & Co. Ltd., 18 Bedford Row, London WC1. .

Grant Educational Co. Ltd., 91 Union Street, Glasgow.

George Harrap & Co. Ltd., 182 High Holborn, London WC1V 7AX.

Rupert Hart-Davis, 3 Upper James Street, Golden Square, London W1.

Heinemann Educational Books Ltd., 48 Charles Street, Mayfair, London W1.

Holmes McDougall, 30 Royal Terrace, Edinburgh 7.

Thomas Hope & Sankey Hudson Ltd., Ashton's Mill, Chapel-town Street, Manchester M1 2NH.

Hulton Educational Publications Ltd., Raans Road, Amersham, Bucks.

Initial Teaching Publishing Co. Ltd., 9 Southampton Place, London WC1.

Longman Group Ltd., Longman House, Burnt Mill, Harlow, Essex.

Macdonald & Co. Ltd., St. Giles House, 49/50 Poland Street, London W1.

McGraw-Hill, Shoppenhangers Road, Maidenhead, Berks.

Macmillan & Co. Ltd., Brunel Road, Basingstoke, Hants.

Methuen & Eyre & Spottiswoode Ltd., 11 New Fetter Lane, London EC4.

Frederick Muller Ltd., 110 Fleet Street, London EC4.

National Foundation for Educational Research, The Mere, Upton Park, Slough.

Thomas Nelson & Sons, 36 Park Street, London W1.

George Newnes, 88 Kingsway, London WC2B 6AB.

James Nisbet & Co. Ltd., Digswell Place, Welwyn, Herts.

Oliver & Boyd Ltd., Tweeddale Court, 14 High Street, Edinburgh 1.

Oxford University Press, 37 Dover Street, London W1X 4AH.

Pergamon Press Ltd., Headington Hill Hall, Oxford. ·

Philip & Tacey Ltd., 201 High Street, New Malden, Surrey.

Rank-REC Ltd., Millbank Tower, Millbank, London SW1.

Reader's Digest, 25 Berkeley Square, London W1.

Remedial Supply Co., Dixon Street, Wolverhampton, Staffs.

Science Research Associates Ltd., Reading Road, Henley-on-Thames, Oxford.

Schofield & Sims Ltd., 35 St. John's Road, Huddersfield, Yorks.

Scott, Foresman & Co., 32 West Street, Brighton BN1 2RT.

Stillit Books Ltd., 72 New Bond Street, London W1.

University of London Press Ltd., St. Paul's House, Warwick Lane, London EC4.

Visigraph Ltd., Bromyard, Herefordshire.

Ward Lock Educational, 116 Baker Street, London W1.

Frederick Warne & Co. Ltd., 40 Bedford Square, London WC1.

Weston Woods Studios Ltd., PO Box 2, Henley-on-Thames, Oxford.

Wheaton & Co., Headington Hill Hall, Oxford OX3 0BW.

Wills & Hepworth Ltd., PO Box 12, Derby Square, Loughborough, Leicestershire.

Glossary

Aphasia   Disorder of the speech function.

Aphrasia   Inability to speak connected phrases, though able to utter separate sounds.

Articulatory   Relating to clarity of speech.

Asymbolia   Inability to use or understand language because of cerebral disorder.

Audile   Term used for a type of individual who relies mainly on auditory imagery.

Auditory acuity   Sharpness of hearing.

Auditory discrimination   Ability to detect differences and similarities in words.

Auditory memory   Ability to remember a sound which has been perceived.

Auditory perception   Awareness of a sound sensation.

Aural   Relating to the ear, but frequently equivalent to auditory.

Blending   Bringing together the constituent sounds of a word in order to form the whole word.

Cerebral dominance   One side of the body is usually preferred to the other—one area of the brain appears to determine a person's preference.

Compensatory education Education to meet the needs of disadvantaged or under-priviledged children.

Configuration The general outline of a word.

Contextual clues Assistance in reading obtained from other words in the text.

Controlled vocabulary Introduction of new words in a book is controlled to prevent the child having too many words to memorise—level of difficulty is controlled.

Cross laterality A lack of established dominance—there may be a different hand dominance from eye dominance, e.g. a left-eyed person who is right-handed.

Diacritical marks Marks used to assist the reader in making the correct sounds for symbols.

Diagnosis Searching for the nature, cause and extent of a child's weakness or disability.

Digraphs Two letters which combine to make one sound, e.g. wh, ee.

Diphthongs Two vowels representing one vowel sound, e.g. ou, oi, oy.

Dyslexia Severe reading disability—suggested by some to be the result of brain damage—may be referred to as word blindness.

Dysphasia Any impairment of the language function—due to brain lesion.

Eyedness Referring to the preferred or leading eye.

Fixation Focusing of the eye upon a word or group of words.

Flash cards Cards of words, phrases or sentences which are briefly exposed to encourage the child's word recognition.

Gestalt Refers to form, structure or integrated whole.

Graded reading scheme   A series of early reading books in which the vocabulary is controlled in order of difficulty.

Graphemes   Letters of the alphabet.

Handedness   Referring to the preferred hand.

Innate   Present in the individual at birth—generally implies inheritance.

Intelligence quotient   Ratio of mental age to chronological age—expressed as a percentage.

Inversion   A term used when an individual sees a letter upside down.

i.t.a.   initial teaching alphabet.

Kinaesthetic   Using the sense of touch and movement.

Language experience approach   An approach to the teaching of reading based on the child's own experiences—vocabulary is drawn from the child's spoken words and from his written work.

Left/right orientation   The ability to read from left to right.

Linguistic approach   A method of teaching reading with words graded according to the complexity of their spelling.

'Look and say'   The method of reading using sight words.

Maladjustment   The condition of an individual who is unable to adapt or adjust himself adequately to his physical, occupational or social environment—usually with repercussions on his emotional life.

Maturation   This involves the process of growth as opposed to the process of learning.

Mental age   Intelligence expressed in relation to the intelligence graded by age of the total population.

Mirror writing Writing produced in the laterally reverse direction—from right to left—this appears as normal when seen in a mirror.

Mixed method The teaching of reading involving a number of methods, e.g. 'look and say', phonic and sentence methods.

Myopia Short-sightedness.

Orthography Spelling.

Perception Awareness and interpretation of incoming stimuli.

Phonemes Sound-units.

Phonetics A phonetic language is one where there is perfect consistency between symbol and sound.

Phonic method The teaching of reading when the emphasis is placed upon the sounds of letters.

Primer A first reading book.

Readiness The level of development necessary to successfully begin a new learning task.

Reading age A child's reading attainment when compared with the reading standard of the average child.

Retardation A term frequently used when a child's attainments fall below his ability.

Reversal Reversing a letter or word, e.g. on for no, was for saw, d for b.

Sight vocabulary The number of words an individual can recognise in print.

Sight words Words learned by sight and not by building them up sound by sound.

Specific abilities Abilities involved in some but not all tasks.

Stammering A series of irregular hesitations and repetitions in speech—used as synonymous with stuttering.

Strephosymbolia The perceiving of objects reversed as in mirror images.

Supplementary material Books or apparatus used to reinforce the learning of tasks involved in a basic reading scheme.

Synthesis The joining of constituent sounds to form a whole word.

Tachistoscope A device for controlling the length of time a flash card is displayed.

T.o. Traditional orthography—the usual spelling of English words.

Visile An individual whose imagery is predominantly visual.

Visual acuity The sharpness of vision.

Visual discrimination The ability to detect differences and similarities in shape, size and colour.

Visual memory The ability to remember a visual image.

Visual perception The ability to be aware of an image which falls on the retina.

Word blindness Severe reading disability—may be referred to as dyslexia.

Word building Building up a word from its letters and sounds.

Word recognition The ability to recognise a printed word.

References

Ace, P. W. (1956), 'A remedial teaching scheme', *Brit. J. Educ. Psychol.*, 26, 3, 191.

Armstrong, H. G. (1965), 'Special educational treatment in the ordinary schools', *Brit. J. Educ. Psychol*, 35, 2, 242–244.

Austin, M. C. (1953), *Identifying Readers who Need Corrective Instruction* (Supplementary Educational Monograph No. 79), University of Chicago Press.

Baldwin, G. (1969), *Patterns of Sound*, Chartwell Press.

Battin, R. R. and Haugh, C. O. (1964), *Speech and Language Delay*, Charles C. Thomas.

Beck, J. (1968), *How to Raise a Brighter Child*, Souvenir Press.

Belmont, L. and Birch, A. G. (1965), 'Lateral dominance, lateral awareness, and reading disability', *Child Development*, 36, 57–71.

Benton, A. L. (1959), *Right-Left Discrimination and Finger Localisation*, Hoeber & Harper.

Benton, A. L. in Money, J. (1962), *Reading Disability : Progress and Research Needs in Dyslexia*, The Johns Hopkins Press.

Bernstein, B. (1961), 'Aspects of language and learning in the genesis of the social process', *J. Child Psychology & Psychiatry*, 1, 315–324.

Betts, E. A. (1950), *Foundations of Reading Instruction*, American Book Co.

Birch, A. G. in Money, J. (1962), *Reading Disability : Progress and Research Needs in Dyslexia*, The Johns Hopkins Press.

Bleasdale, E. and W. (1967), *Reading by Rainbow*, Moor Platt Press.

Bloomfield, L. and Barnhart, C. L. (1961), *Let's Read: A Linguistic Approach*, Wayne State University Press.

Bowlby, J. (1965), *Child Care and the Growth of Love*, Penguin.

Boyce, E. R. (1959), *The Gay Way Series*, Macmillan.

232

Bramwyche, C. (1972), 'Listening Tests', *Times Educational Supplement*, 11 February.

Briggs, R. F. (1966), 'The language of culturally deprived children', *Forward Trends*, 10, 3, 61–69.

Brimer, M. A. and Dunn, L. M. (1963), *English Picture Vocabulary Test*, NFER.

Brown, R. I. and Bookbinder, G. E. (1969), *The Clifton Audio/Visual Reading Programme*, ESA.

Bruce, J. D. (1964), 'The analysis of word sounds by young children', *Brit. J. Educ. Psychol*, 34, 2, 158–169.

Burroughs, G. E. R. (1957), *The Study of the Vocabulary of Young Children*, Oliver & Boyd.

Burt, C. (1925), *The Young Delinquent*, ULP.

Burt, C. (1946), *The Backward Child*, ULP.

Burt, C. (1950), *The Backward Child*, ULP.

Burt, C. (1953), 2nd Edit. *The Causes and Treatment of Backwardness*, ULP.

Burt, C. *Graded Word Reading Test*, ULP.

Carmichael, L. (1954), Ed. *Manual of Child Psychology*, Chapman & Hall.

Cashdan, A., Pumfrey, P. D. and Lunzer, E. A. (1971), 'Children receiving remedial teaching in reading', *Educ. Res.*, 13, 2, 98–105.

Cass, J. E. (1967), *Literature and the Young Child*, Longman.

Chall, J. (1967), *Learning to Read : The Great Debate*, McGraw-Hill.

Chazan, M. (1962), 'School Phobia', *Brit. J. Educ. Psychol.*, 32, 209–217.

Clark, M. M. (1957), *Left Handedness*, ULP.

Clark, M. M. (1970), *Reading Difficulties in Schools*, Penguin.

Collins, J. (1961), *The Effects of Remedial Education*, Oliver & Boyd.

Cooper, M. G. (1966a), 'School refusal', *Educ. Res.*, 8, 2, 115–127.

Cooper, M. G. (1966b), 'School refusal: an inquiry into the part played by school and home', *Educ. Res.*, 8, 3, 223–229.

Crichton Vocabulary Scale, H. K. Lewis.

Critchley, M. (1964), *The Dyslexic Child*, Heinemann Medical Books.

Curr, W. & Gourlay, N. (1960), 'The effect of practice on performance tests', *Brit. J. Educ. Psychol*, 30, 2, 155–167.

Curry, L. R. (1962), 'The effects of socio-economic status on the scholastic achievement of sixth-grade children', *Brit. J. Educ. Psychol.*, 32, 46–49.

Daniels, J. C. and Diack, H. (1958), *The Standard Reading Tests,* Chatto & Windus.

Daniels, J. C. and Diack, H. (1967), *The Royal Road Readers,* Chatto & Windus.

Daniels, J. C. and Diack, H. (1967), *The Royal Road Readers Teacher's Book,* Chatto & Windus.

Davie, R., Butler, N. and Goldstein, H. (1972), *From Birth to Seven,* Longman.

Department of Education and Science, (1966), *Progress in Reading,* Educ. Pamph. No. 50, HMSO.

Department of Education and Science, (1964), *The Use of Books,* HMSO.

Department of Education and Science, (1967), *Children and their Primary Schools, (Plowden Report),* HMSO.

Department of Education and Science, (1967), *The School Library,* HMSO.

Diack, H. (1960), *Reading and the Psychology of Perception,* Peter Skinner.

Doll, E. A. (1953), *The Measurement of Social Competence,* Educational Test Bureau, Educational Publishers, USA.

Doman, G. (1965), *Teach Your Baby to Read,* Jonathan Cape.

Douglas, J. W. B. (1964), *The Home and the School,* MacGibbon & Kee.

Douglas, J. W. B. and Ross, J. M. (1965), 'The effects of absence on primary school performance', *Brit. J. Educ. Psychol.,* 35, 28–40.

Downing, J. (1963), *The Downing Readers,* Initial Teaching Publishing Co. Ltd.

Downing, J. (1963), 'Is a "Mental Age of Six" essential for reading readiness?' *Educ. Res.,* 6, 16–28.

Downing, J. (1966), *The i.t.a. Symposium,* NFER.

Downing, J. (1966) Ed., *The First International Reading Symposium,* Cassell.

Downing, J. (1968), 'Should today's children start reading earlier?' in *The Third International Reading Symposium,* Cassell.

Dunham, J. (1960), 'The effects of Remedial Education on Young Children's Reading Ability and Attitude to Reading', *Brit. J. Educ. Psychol.,* 30, 2, 173–175.

Durrell, D. (1956), *Improving Reading Instruction,* World Book Co.

Fernald, G. M. (1943), *Remedial Techniques in the Basic School Subjects,* McGraw-Hill.

Fisher, M. (1964), *Intent Upon Reading,* Brockhampton Press.

Flesch, R. (1955), *Why Johnny Can't Read,* Harper.

France, N. (1964), 'The use of group tests of ability and attainment: a follow-up study from primary to secondary school', *Brit. J. Educ. Psychol.*, 34, 1, 19–33.

Fraser, E. (1959), *Home Environment and the School*, ULP.

Fries, C. C. (1962), *Linguistics and Reading*, Holt, Rinehart & Winston.

Galt Reading Materials, Brookfield Road, Cheadle, Cheshire.

Gates, A. (1947), *The Improvement of Reading*, Macmillan, New York.

Gattegno, C. (1962), *Words in Colour*, Educational Explorers.

Gattegno, C. (1962), *Words in Colour*, Cuisenaire Co.

Gesell, N. (1954), *The Child from Five to Ten*, Methuen.

Goodacre, E. J. (1967a), *Teaching Beginners to Read : Report No. 1 Reading in Infant Classes*, NFER.

Goodacre, E. J. (1967b), *Teaching Beginners to Read : Report No. 2 Teachers and their Pupils' Home Background*, NFER.

Goodacre, E. J. (1970), 'Reading 1: What the teachers want', *Times Educational Supplement*, 27 November.

Gulliford, R. (1969), *Backwardness and Educational Failure*, NFER.

Grassam, E. H. (1966), *Phonic Workbooks*, Ginn.

Hardiment, M., Hicks, J. and Kremer, T. (1969), *Wordmaster Major*, Macdonald.

Harris, D. B. (1957), *The Concept of Development*, University of Minnesota Press.

Hersov, L. (1960), 'Persistent non-attendance at school'. Also 'Refusal to go to school', *J. Child Psychology & Psychiatry*, 1, 130–136, 137–145.

Hillman, H. H. and Snowdon, R. C. (1960), 'Part-Time Classes for Young Backward Readers', *Brit. J. Educ. Psychol.*, 30, 2, 168–172.

Hinshelwood, J. (1895), 'Word-blindness and visual memory', *Lancet*, 2, 1564–70.

Houghton and Daniels (1966), *Bulletin of the United Kingdom Reading Association*, July.

Hughes, J. M. (1969), 'Learning to read with the tape recorder', *Times Educational Supplement*, 23 May.

Hughes, J. M. (1969), 'The tape recorder as a reading aid', *Teachers World*, 15 August.

Hughes, J. M. (1970), *Aids to Reading*, Evans Brothers.

Hughes, J. M. (1969), *Beginning Reading*, Evans Brothers.

Hughes, J. M. (1972), *Moving on with Reading*, Nelson.

235

Hughes, J. M. (1972), *Phonics and the Teaching of Reading*, Evans Brothers.

Hughes, J. M. (1973), *Reading with Phonics*, Evans Brothers.

Hughes, J. M. and Presland, J. L. (1969), 'Applied Psychology and Backward Readers', Supplement to *Journal and Newsletter*, 2, 4 (Association of Ed. Psychologists).

Ingram, T. T. S. (1960), 'Paediatric aspects of specific developmental dysphasia, dyslexia and dysgraphia', *Cerebral Palsy Bull.*, 2, 254–276.

Inner London Education Authority (1963–7), Report on the use of the Initial Teaching Alphabet in a sample of London schools.

Isle of Wight Survey (1965), Sponsored by the DES, Association for the Aid of Crippled Children and the Medical Research Council.

Jackson, S. (1967), *The Teacher's Guide to Tests and Testing*, Longman.

Jackson, S. (1971), *Get Reading Right*, Gibson.

Johnson, D. J. and Myklebust, H. R. (1967), *Learning Disabilities*, Grune & Stratton.

Jones, C. H. (1968), *From Left to Right*, Autobates Learning Systems.

Jones, J. G. (1962), *Teaching with Tape*, The Focal Press.

Jones, J. K. (1965), 'Colour as an aid to visual perception in early reading', *Brit. J. Educ. Psychol.*, 35, 1, 21–27.

Jones, J. K. (1967), *Colour Story Reading*, Nelson.

Jones, J. K. (1967), *Research Report on Colour Story Reading*, Nelson.

Jones, W. R. (1965), *Step Up and Read*, ULP.

Kahn, J. H. (1958), 'School refusal', *Medical Officer*, 100, 337 (Reprint obtained from Dr Kahn).

Kahn, J. H. (1963), 'School phobia', *Lancet*, 1, 821 (Reprint obtained from Dr Kahn).

Kawi, A. A. and Pasamanick, B. (1959), *Prenatal and Paranatal Factors in the Development of Childhood Reading Disorders*, Monographs of the Society for Research in Child Development, No. 73.

Keir, G. (1947), *Adventures in Reading*, OUP.

Keir, G. (1951), *Teachers' Manual to Adventures in Reading*, OUP.

Kellmer-Pringle, M. L. and Gulliford, R. (1953), 'A note on "An evaluation of remedial education" ', *Brit. J. Educ. Psychol.*, 23, 196–199.

Kellmer-Pringle, M. L. *et al.* (1966a), *11,000 Seven-Year Olds*,

Longman.

Kellmer-Pringle, M. L. (1966b), *Deprivation and Education,* Longman.

Kellmer-Pringle, M. L. (1966c), *Social Learning and its Measurement,* Longman.

Kinder, R. L. F. (1970), 'Learning to Listen', in *Reading Skills,* UKRA, Ward Lock Educational.

Kirk, S. A. and McCarthy, J. (1961), *Illinois Test of Psycholinguistic Abilities,* University of Illinois.

Krausen, R. (1972), 'The relationship of certain "pre-reading" skills 'to general ability and social class in nursery children', *Educ. Res.,* 15, 1, 72–79.

Language Master, Bell & Howell, Wembley.

Lewis, M. M. (1963), *Language, Thought and Personality in Infancy and Childhood,* Harrap.

Lewis, M. M. (1969), *Language and the Child,* NFER.

Library Association, Books for Young People (Group 1).

Lovell, K. (1963), *Educational Psychology and Children,* ULP.

Lovell, K. *et al.* (1962), 'A summary of a study of the reading ages of children who had received remedial teaching', *Brit. J. Educ. Psychol.,* 32, 66–71.

Lovell, K. *et al.* (1963), 'A further study of the educational progress of children who had received remedial education', *Brit. J. Educ. Psychol.,* 33, 1, 3–9.

Lovell, K. *et al.* (1964), 'A study of some cognitive and other disabilities in backward readers of average intelligence as assessed by a non-verbal test', *Brit. J. Educ. Psychol.,* 34, 58–64.

Luria, A. R. (1961), *The Role of Speech in the Regulation of Normal and Subnormal Behaviour,* Pergamon.

Lynn, R. (1963), 'Reading Readiness 11—Reading readiness and the perceptual abilities of young children', *Educ. Res.,* 6, 10–15.

MacKay, D., Thompson, B. and Schauh, P. (1970), *Breakthrough to Literacy,* Longman for the Schools Council.

Malmquist, E. (1958), *Factors related to Reading Disabilities in the First Grade of the Elementary School,* Almquist & Wiksell, Stockholm.

Mason, G. E. and Prater, N. J. (1966), 'Early reading and reading instruction', *Elementary English,* 43, 483–488 and 527.

McLaren, V. M. (1950), *Socio-economic Status and Reading Ability—A Study in Infant Reading,* Studies in Reading, Vol. 2, ULP.

McCullagh, S. K. (1959), *The Griffin Readers,* E. J. Arnold.

McCullough, C. M. *et al.* (1946), *Problems in the Improvement of Reading,* McGraw-Hill, New York.

McKee, P., Harrison, M. L., McCowen, A. and Lehr, E. (1955), *The McKee Reading Scheme,* Nelson.

McNally, J. and Murray, W. (1962), *Key Words to Literacy,* Schoolmaster Publishing Co. Ltd.

McNeil, J. D. and Keislar, E. R. (1963), 'Value of the oral response in beginning reading: an experimental study using programmed instruction', *Brit. J. Educ. Psychol.,* 33, 2, 162–168.

Melser, J. (1969), *Read it Yourself Books,* Methuen.

Merritt, J. E. (1964), 'The linguistic approach to reading', In *The Third International Reading Symposium,* Cassell.

Millard, C. V. (1958), *Child Growth in the Elementary School Years,* Heath & Co., Boston.

Money, J. (1962), Ed., *Reading Disability : Progress and Research Needs in Dyslexia,* The Johns Hopkins Press.

Monroe, M. (1946), *Children who Cannot Read,* University of Chicago Press.

Morris, J. M. (1959), *Reading in the Primary School,* Newnes.

Morris, J. M. (1969), *Standards and Progress in Reading,* NFER.

Mosely, D. (1971), *The English Colour Code Programmed Reading Course,* National Society for Mentally Handicapped Children.

Mosher, M. (1966), *Times Educational Supplement,* 11 February.

Moxon, C. A. V. (1962), *A Remedial Reading Method,* Metheun.

Moyle, D. (1968), *The Teaching of Reading,* Ward Lock Educational.

Murray, W. (1964), *The Ladybird Key Words Reading Scheme,* Wills & Hepworth.

National Book League, *Four to Fourteen,* Cambridge University Press.

National Union of Teachers (1969), *The Future of Teacher Education.*

Neale, M. D. (1958), *Neale Analysis of Reading Ability,* Macmillan.

O'Donnell, M. and Munro, R. (1951), *Janet and John Reading Scheme,* Nisbet.

Olson, W. C. (1959), *Child Development,* Heath & Co., Boston.

Parker, D. H. *Reading Laboratory Series,* Science Research Associates.

Peabody Language Developments Kits, (1965), American Guidance Service.

Peters, M. (1967), *Spelling : Caught or Taught?* Routledge &

Kegan Paul.

Pidgeon, D. A. (1960), 'A national survey of the ability and attainment of children at three age levels', *Brit. J. Educ. Psychol.*, 30, 1, 13–31.

Prechtl, in Money (1962) Ed., *Reading Disability: Progress and Research Needs in Dyslexia*, The Johns Hopkins Press.

Primary Audio Set (Headphones), S. G. Brown Ltd., Watford.

Rabinovitch, in Money, J. (1962) Ed., *Reading Disability: Progress and Research Needs*, The Johns Hopkins Press.

Randell, B. (1966), *Methuen Caption Books*, Methuen.

Reed, G. F. (1966), 'The association of auditory high frequency with verbal and written comprehension and expression', *Brit. J. Educ. Psychol.*, 36, 1, 118–121.

Reid, J. F. (1968), 'Dyslexia: a problem of communication', *Educ. Res.*, 10, 2, 126–133.

Reis, M. (1962), *Fun with Phonics*, Cambridge Art Publishers.

Remedial Supply Company, Dixon Street, Wolverhampton.

Report of the Advisory Committee on Handicapped Children, (1972), Children with Specific Reading Difficulties, HMSO.

Richardson, S. (1956), 'Some evidence relating to the validity of selection for grammar schools', *Brit. J. Educ. Psychol.*, 26, 15–24.

Roberts, G. R. (1960), 'A study of motivation in remedial reading', *Brit. J. Educ. Psychol.*, 30, 2, 176–179.

Roberts, G. R. (1969), *Reading in Primary Schools*, Routledge & Kegan Paul.

Robinson, H. M. (1953), *Problems of Corrective Reading* (Supplementary Educational Monograph No. 79), University of Chicago Press.

Sampson, O. C. (1962), 'Reading skill at eight years in relation to speech and other factors', *Brit. J. Educ. Psychol.*, 32, 12–17.

Sampson, O. C. (1966), 'Reading and adjustment: A review of the literature', *Educ. Res.*, 8, 3, 184–190.

Sampson, O. C. (1969), 'Remedial education services', *Remedial Education*, 4, 3–8 and 61–65.

Schonell, F. J. (1948a), *Backwardness in the Basic Subjects*, Oliver & Boyd.

Schonell, F. J. (1948b), *The Psychology and Teaching of Reading*, Oliver & Boyd.

Schonell, F. J., Serjeant, I. and Flowerdew, P. (1958), *The Happy Venture Readers*, Oliver & Boyd.

Schonell, F. J. (1961), *The Psychology and Teaching of Reading*, Oliver & Boyd.

Schonell, F. J., *Graded Word Reading Test,* Oliver & Boyd.

Schonell, F. J. and Wall, W. D. (1949), *Remedial Education Centre,* (First Annual Report, University of Birmingham).

School Library Association, Primary School Books.

Shearer, E. (1967), 'The Long-Term Effects of Remedial Education', *Educ. Res.,* 9, 3, 219–222.

Southgate, V. (1958), *Southgate Group Reading Tests,* ULP.

Southgate, V. (1965), 'Approaching i.t.a. results with caution', *Educ. Res.,* 7, 2, 83–96.

Southgate, V. (1967), 'A few comments on 'reading drive', *Educ. Res.,* 9, 2, 145–146.

Southgate, V. (1968), *First Words,* Macmillan.

Southgate, V. and Havenhand, J. (1961), *Sounds and Words,* ULP.

Southgate, V. and Roberts, G. R. (1970), *Reading—which approach?* ULP.

Spooncer, F. A., *Group Reading Test,* ULP.

Stott, D. H. (1958), *The Social Adjustment of Children,* ULP.

Stott, D. H. (1962), *Programmed Reading Kit* (Revised 1972), Holmes McDougall.

Stott, D. H. (1962), *Manual for the Programmed Reading Kit* (Revised 1972), Holmes McDougall.

Stott, D. H. (1964), *Roads to Literacy,* Holmes McDougall.

Stott, D. H. (1966), *Studies of Troublesome Children,* Tavistock Pub.

Sunday Times Magazine, (1966), Williams, P. 30 October.

Sutton, M. H. (1966), 'First grade children who learn to read in Kindergarten', *Reading Teacher,* 19, 192–196.

Swansea Test of Phonic Skills, (1971), Blackwell.

Tanner, J. M. (1961), *Education and Physical Growth,* ULP.

Tansley, A. E. (1960), *Sound Sense,* E. J. Arnold.

Tansley, A. E. (1967), *Reading and Remedial Reading,* Routledge & Kegan Paul.

Tansley, A. E. and Nicholls, R. H. (1962), *Racing to Read,* E. J. Arnold.

Taylor, J. and Ingleby, T. (1965), *This is the Way I Go,* Longman.

Taylor, J. and Ingleby, T. (1966), *Reading with Rhythm,* Longman.

Thackray, D. V. (1965), 'The relationship between reading readiness and reading progress', *Brit. J. Educ. Psychol.,* 35, 252–254.

Times Educational Supplement, (1966), Mosher, M. 11 February.

Times Educational Supplement, (1972), 'Listening Tests', Bramwyche, C. 11 February.

Times Educational Supplement, (1970), 'Reading: What the teachers want', Goodacre, E. J. 27 November.

Trease, G. *Tales Out of School,* Heinemann.

Valentine, C. V. (1953), *Introduction to Experimental Psychology,* London University Tutorial Press.

Vernon, M. D. (1957), *Backwardness in Reading,* CUP.

Vernon, M. D. (1960), 'The Investigation of Reading Problems Today', *Brit. J. Educ. Psychol.,* 30, 2, 146–154.

Vernon, M. D. (1962), 'Specific Dyslexia', *Brit. J. Educ. Psychol.,* 32, 143–150.

Vernon, P. E. *Graded Word Reading Test,* ULP.

Vernon, P. E. (1948), (a) 'A preliminary investigation of the vocabulary of Scottish children entering school.' (b) 'Word counts of infant readers.' Scottish Council for Research in Education, *Studies in Reading Vol. 1,* ULP.

Vernon, P. E. (1953), *Personality Tests and Assessments,* Methuen.

Vernon, P. E. (1960), *Intelligence and Attainment Tests,* ULP.

Warburton, F. W. and Southgate, V. (1969), *i.t.a. An Independent Evaluation,* W. and R. Chambers and J. Murray.

Watts, A. F. (1948), *Language and Mental Development of Children,* Harrap.

Watts, A. F. *Holborn Reading Scale,* Harrap.

Watts, A. F. *Sentence Reading Test,* NFER.

Wepman, J. M. (1958), *Auditory Discrimination Test,* distributed by NFER.

Weston, J. (1968), *The Tape Recorder in the Classroom,* National Committee for Audio/Visual Aids in Education.

Weston Woods Filmstrips, distributed by Children's Book Centre, London.

Williams, J. D. (1965), 'Some problems involved in the experimental comparison of teaching methods', *Educ. Res.* 8, 1, 26–41.

Williams, P. (1961), 'The growth of reading vocabulary and some of its implications', *Brit. J. Educ. Psychol.,* 31, 104–105.

Wisenthal, M. (1965), 'Sex differences in attitudes and attainment in junior schools', *Brit. J. Educ. Psychol.,* 35, 1, 79–85.

Yardley, A. (1970), *Exploration and Language,* Evans Bros.

Zangwill, O. L. (1960), *Cerebral Dominance and its Relation to Psychological Function,* Oliver & Boyd.

Index